THE ENCYCLOPEDIA OF
Pastel Techniques

Judy Martin

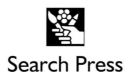

Search Press

A QUARTO BOOK

This edition published in 2017 by
Search Press Ltd.
Wellwood, North Farm Road
Tunbridge Wells
Kent, TNR 3DR
United Kingdom

Previously published by Search Press Ltd.
as *The Encyclopedia of Pastel Techniques*
in 2009.

Copyright © 2009, 2017
Quarto Publishing plc

ISBN: 978-1-78221-594-3

Conceived, designed and produced by
Quarto Publishing plc
an imprint of The Quarto Group
The Old Brewery
6 Blundell Street
London N7 9BH
www.quartoknows.com

QUAR:EPPN

Printed in China

10 9 8 7 6 5 4 3 2 1

Page 2, Maureen Spinale,
A River Runs Through It

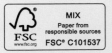

Contents

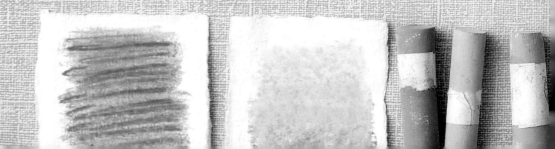

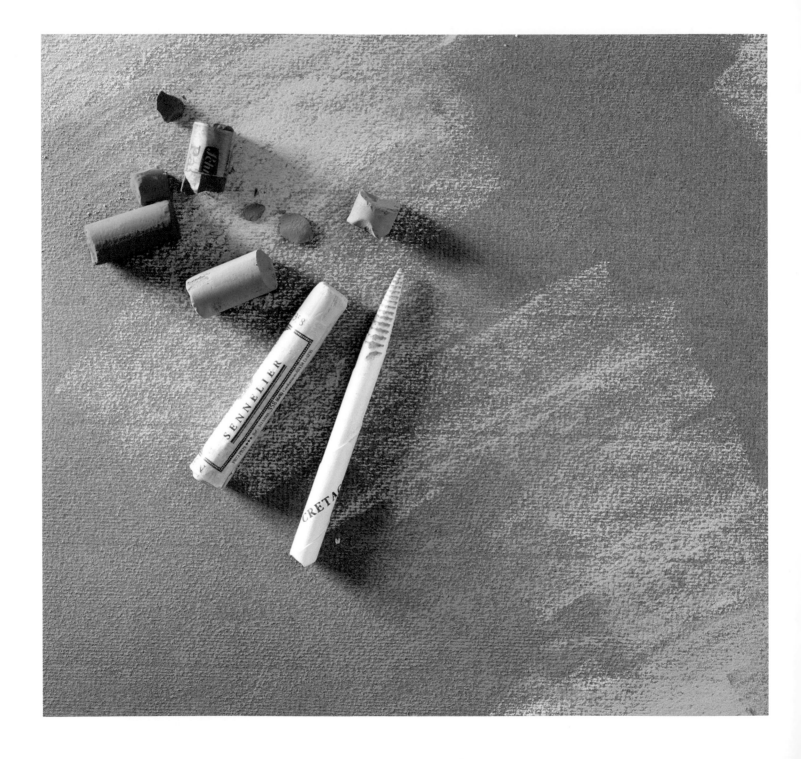

Tools and Techniques

Pastels are unique in the way they bridge the gap between painting and drawing media. The stick form gives pastel strokes a linear character that enables you to exploit the calligraphic qualities of line and the controlled effects of linear shading, while the loose texture and brilliant colour qualities allow for painterly effects of mass and surface texture. Pastel is the most direct of colour media – it flows directly from your hand and, unlike a brush or pen nib, has no intermediary factor that contributes its own qualities to the marks you make. You must juxtapose, mix and blend your colours on the support – you cannot try out colour mixes in a palette or paint out errors and begin again.

To achieve the full potential of pastels, you need to be aware of the medium's technical range and develop confidence in applying it. Practising the individual techniques demonstrated in this section of the book – with no initial pressure to produce a successful or even recognizable image – will enable you to get the feel of the medium, gaining practical experience which will contribute to your ability to interpret a particular subject.

Pastel Types

Many manuals on pastel painting take for granted the use of traditional soft pastels, a dry medium that provides the richness and variety of paint colours. Soft pastel is certainly the most versatile and widely used kind of pastel, but the modern range of materials includes other pastel types that have their own specific characteristics as drawing and painting media, and also function as useful supplements to soft pastels.

The techniques described in this encyclopedia are related to the full pastel range – soft pastels, hard pastels, pastel pencils, oil pastels and water-soluble pastels. The exact characteristics of all of these media vary slightly between different manufacturers' ranges. You may find a particular brand that you prefer for its ease of handling or colour qualities, but it is quite possible to mix and match from different selections, so trying out the range is unlikely to involve acquiring anything that you cannot use. Because the colours are so attractive, it is tempting to pick out multiple hues when you are buying. However, until you are familiar with a particular product, and have tried out its properties for colour mixing and textural variation, it is best to start with a few basic colours, gradually adding to your stock.

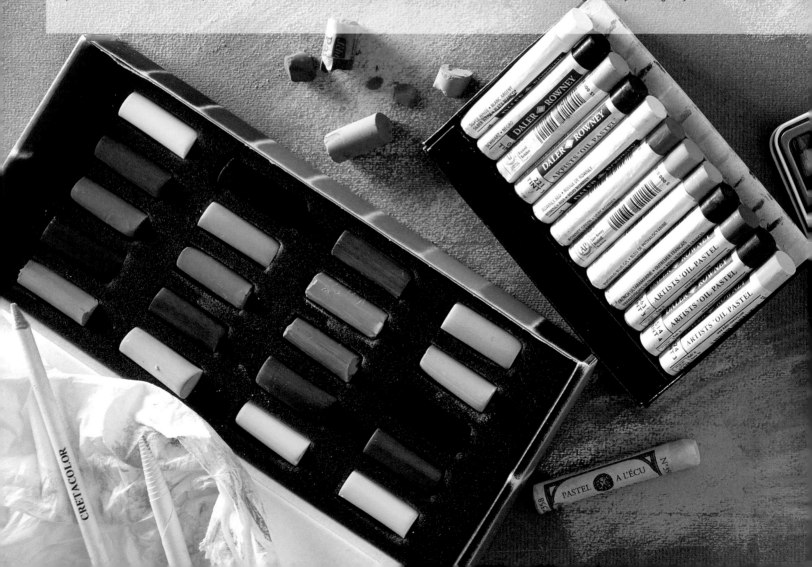

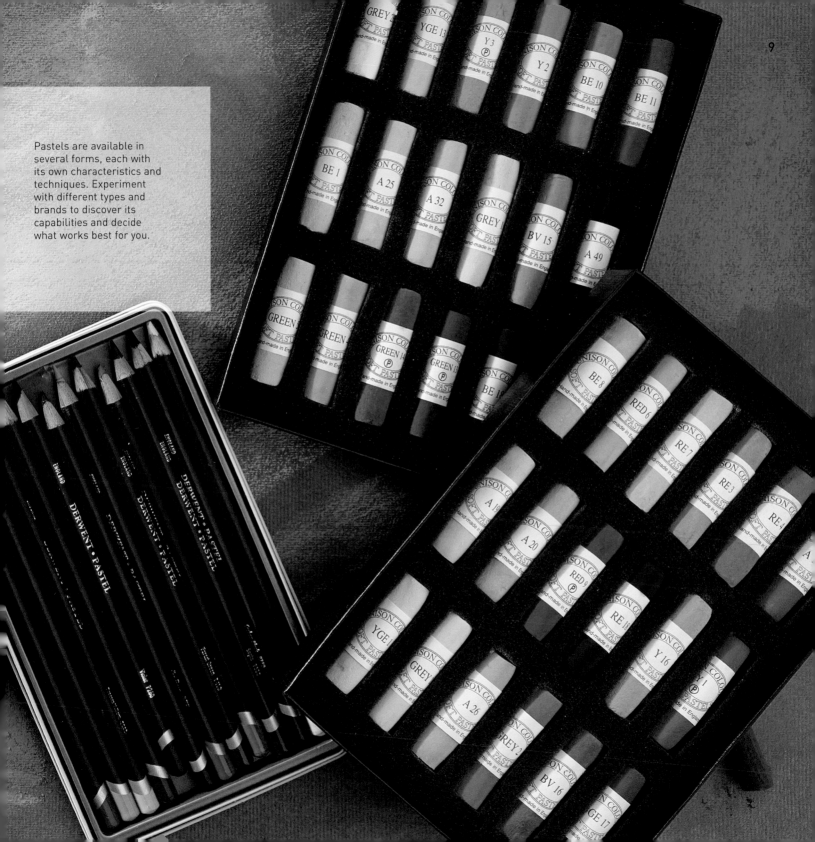

Pastels are available in several forms, each with its own characteristics and techniques. Experiment with different types and brands to discover its capabilities and decide what works best for you.

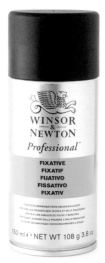

Hard pastels

Soft pastels

The basic ingredients of pastels are ground pigments and a binder that holds the pigment particles together. They are mixed to form a stiff paste, which is then compressed into round- or square-sectioned sticks and allowed to dry. Soft pastels have a high proportion of pigment to binder, hence the ease with which they transfer colour to the support and the brilliance and rich texture of the colours. Soft pastels may also include white chalk, or a similar filler, which gives luminosity to bright hues and pale tints.

The colour ranges vary with the manufacturer, and there is no standard identification of the pigments. Some of the high-quality pastel ranges have literally hundreds of colours, including pure hues together with lighter and darker tones of each individual hue – these may be identified by numerical codes that signify related colour values. This abundance of colours acknowledges the directness of pastel as a painting medium – deprived of the ability to mix colours infinitely as you can with paint, you are offered a palette of pastels that would enable you to vary the colour of every stroke. Other good brands provide slightly less colour variation, but all are likely to meet your requirements more than adequately.

The loose, grainy texture of soft pastels provides great colour clarity, but it is also why many people find pastels difficult to use. The powdery colour can seem to spread uncontrollably, and it is aggravating when a fragile pastel stick snaps or crumbles in the middle of a stroke. This can lead to a cautious approach, but the best results come from working freely and decisively.

Hard pastels

These have a greater proportion of binder to pigment, so they are more stable in use than soft pastels, but do not have such wide potential for varied surface effects. Traditionally, they are used for preliminary sketching out of a composition, and for adding linear detail and "sharpening" touches to soft pastel work – in effect, hard pastels are the drawing medium that complements soft pastels as a painting medium. You can exploit the linear qualities by using the section edge of the stick, or even sharpening it to a point by shaving it with a fine blade, but there are also several techniques you can use to develop effects of massed colour, such as shading, hatching and crosshatching. The colour range is quite limited by comparison with soft pastels, with nothing like the degrees of variation in hue or tone.

Pastel pencils

These are thin sticks of pastel encased in wood, and come in a relatively limited colour range. The "leads" are typically harder than soft pastels, although they may also be somewhat softer than hard pastels. Their main advantage is that they are clean to use and easy to control. As with hard pastels, you can make use of their linear qualities to add crisp finishing touches to a rendering mainly worked in soft pastels.

Oil pastels

This medium is unique among the pastel types, containing an oil binder that makes the texture dense and greasy and the colours slightly less opaque than soft pastels. Typically, the colours are

Spray fixative will help prevent your pastel work from smudging. Apply an even coverage from a distance of about 30cm (12 in).

Soft pastels

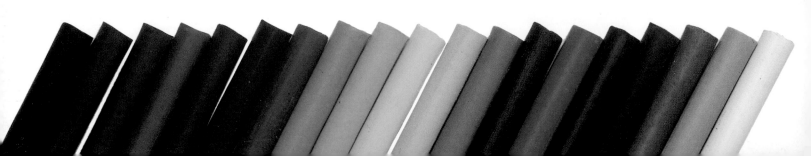

Pastel pencils

Oil pastels

quite strong and the variation of colour values is restricted. The moist texture of oil pastel can quickly fill the grain of the paper, so the capacity to work one colour over another is somewhat limited, but for painting effects, oil pastel marks can be softened and spread by brushing them with turpentine or white spirit.

Water-soluble pastels

The wax content of these colour sticks gives them a slightly moist texture, so that they handle rather like oil pastels when you use them for drawn strokes; but brush over the colour with clean water, and it instantly dissolves into an even, semi-transparent wash. The quality of the wet colour is like a coarse watercolour wash. You can vary it considerably according to the amount of water that you add – for instance, with a barely wetted brush you can spread the colour tint while retaining a strong impression of the linear marks. The restricted colour range is composed of strong, unsubtle hues, but with the potential fluidity of the medium, there is more scope for mixing and blending colours on the working surface.

Extra equipment

Blending stumps (pointed at both ends) and torchons (pointed at only one end) are available in different sizes and are useful for blending colours.

Both pastel pencils and hard pastels are harder than soft pastels. You can buy special sharpening boards containing sheets of fine-grain sandpaper to sharpen the pencils so that you can achieve a fine line.

Use sponges and an applicator to apply, blend and soften pan pastel. Pan pastels offer ultra-soft pastel colour in a cake-like format that can be applied like paint.

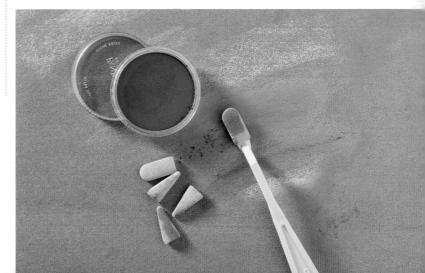

Water-soluble pastels

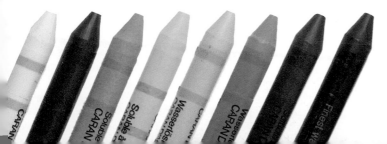

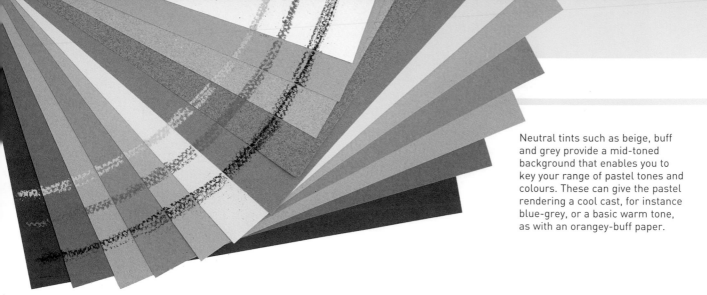

Neutral tints such as beige, buff and grey provide a mid-toned background that enables you to key your range of pastel tones and colours. These can give the pastel rendering a cool cast, for instance blue-grey, or a basic warm tone, as with an orangey-buff paper.

Coloured Grounds

Use of a coloured ground is a traditional aspect of pastel painting, still employed in fresh and interesting ways by contemporary artists. Given that the grainy texture of pastel usually allows the colour of the support to show through, it is not always appropriate that this colour should be white. A coloured ground can be used to set an overall tonal value for the work – dark, medium or light – or to give it a colour bias in terms of warm (beige, buff, brown) or cool (grey, blue, green) colour. It can stand in for a dominant colour in the subject – blue or green for landscape, for example, or buff or terracotta for a townscape.

The wide range of coloured papers available, encompassing varied chromatic qualities and surface textures, provides a wealth of choice for ready-made coloured grounds for pastel work. If you prefer, you can apply colour to a white support using thin washes of watercolour, gouache or acrylic paint, or you can tint a paper subtly with a pastel dry wash. For oil pastel work, you can colour primed paper or canvas board with a glaze of diluted oil paint. In this way, you can achieve the precise colour value you require and grade, blend or texture it if you wish – a coloured ground does not have to be a single or uniform colour.

Colours that are bright or very densely saturated have a strong impact on the overall image, intensifying the hue and texture of the pastel marks.

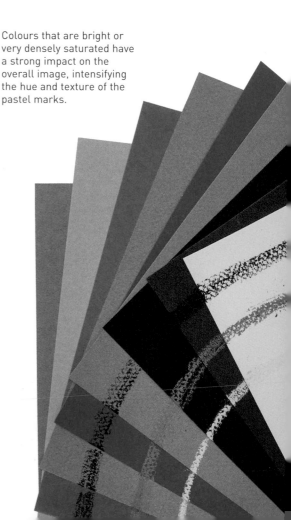

Dark-toned papers enable lighter-tone pastels placed on top to glow. Leaving flecks of dark paper showing through gives life and texture to any blocked-in areas.

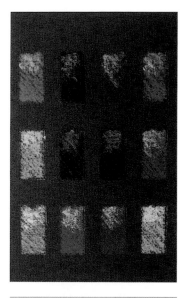
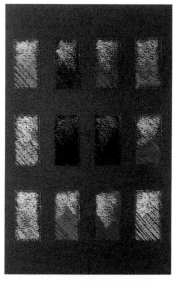
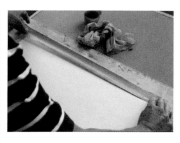
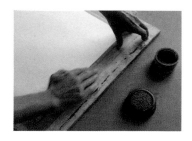

Tinting with watercolour

1 If you are applying a watercolour ground to your paper, it is necessary to stretch it first so it will dry flat after the wet colour has been applied. Soak the paper thoroughly and lay it on a drawing board. Apply a strip of gummed paper tape all along one edge.

2 Smooth down a second strip along the adjacent edge of the paper. Work around all four sides in the same way, making sure there are no wrinkles in the wet paper and pressing the tape down firmly so it adheres well to both paper and board.

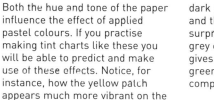
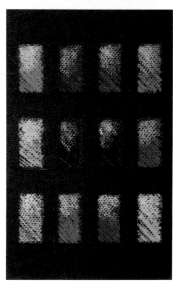
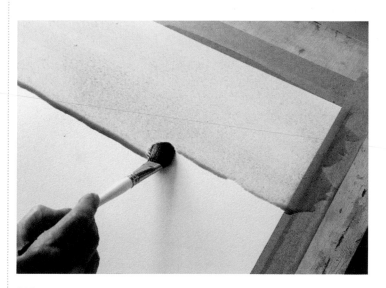

Both the hue and tone of the paper influence the effect of applied pastel colours. If you practise making tint charts like these you will be able to predict and make use of these effects. Notice, for instance, how the yellow patch appears much more vibrant on the dark grey paper than on the buff, and the brown pastel comes up surprisingly light-toned on a dark grey or red ground. The red paper gives greater intensity to the greens, because the colours have complementary contrast.

3 Mix up a large quantity of dilute watercolour in the required colour. Using a large, soft brush, spread an even wash across the paper, working from side to side and gradually extending the wash downward. Allow the paint to dry completely before beginning work in pastel.

Textured Grounds

Some degree of texture on the paper is necessary to successful pastel painting – it needs to have a tooth, or distinct grain, which allows the pastel particles to grip the surface. The colour is unstable on a very smooth surface, and as you build up the pastel strokes they will tend to smear, or fail to adhere. A pronounced paper grain also contributes to the colour qualities of the rendering, since the pastel does not immediately fill the recessed areas of the grain texture, allowing the colour of the paper to show through.

Surfaces suitable for pastel range from cartridge and cover papers, through heavy grained watercolour papers, to mould-made coloured Ingres papers that have an even, visible grain. Fine sandpapers are also sold specifically for pastel work – if you can't obtain them from an art supplier, have a look at the range of abrasive papers in the DIY store. If you are combining pastel with oil or acrylic paint, you can use artist's canvas or canvas board as a working surface. Quite humble materials can also be sympathetic for pastel work, such as cardboard and rough brown wrapping paper.

A kneaded eraser and a selection of blending tools (shown here: stumps, torchons and a silicone-tipped blending tool) are invaluable in pastel painting. Depending on your style of work, you may also find metal stencils useful for very fine detail.

On these swatches of various pastel papers and card, variations in the pressure of the pastel strokes is used to create visual contrast between solid and broken colour. Single-colour and two- or three-colour blends are used to bring out the quality of the various textures. A build-up of thick colour makes the paper grain less distinct.

1, 2 and 3 These surfaces have a very subtle tooth with an even pattern, the pastel blends in, creating smooth, veil-like marks (Daler Rowney Canford paper).
4, 5 and 6 This paper has a linear texture with a strong single direction (Clairefontaine Ingres paper).
7 and 8 This has a canvas-like cross-hatched grain (Canson).
9 and 10 Here, a lovely velvety surface to work on is provided, as the pastel glides onto the surface evenly (Clairefontaine Pastelmat board).
11 Slightly coarse pastel paper gives a granular texture compared to those above.
12 Brown wrapping paper
13 Card
14 Corrugated card
15 Wet and dry 800 sandpaper
16 Hot-pressed watercolour paper
17 Cold-pressed watercolour paper
18 Variegated watercolour wash on a toned ground
19 Rough watercolour paper has strong surface pattern, and is generally suitable for larger pastel work.

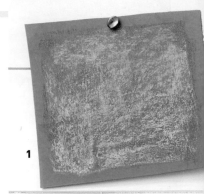

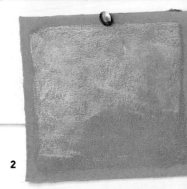

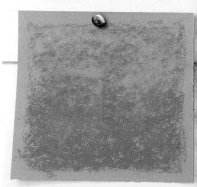

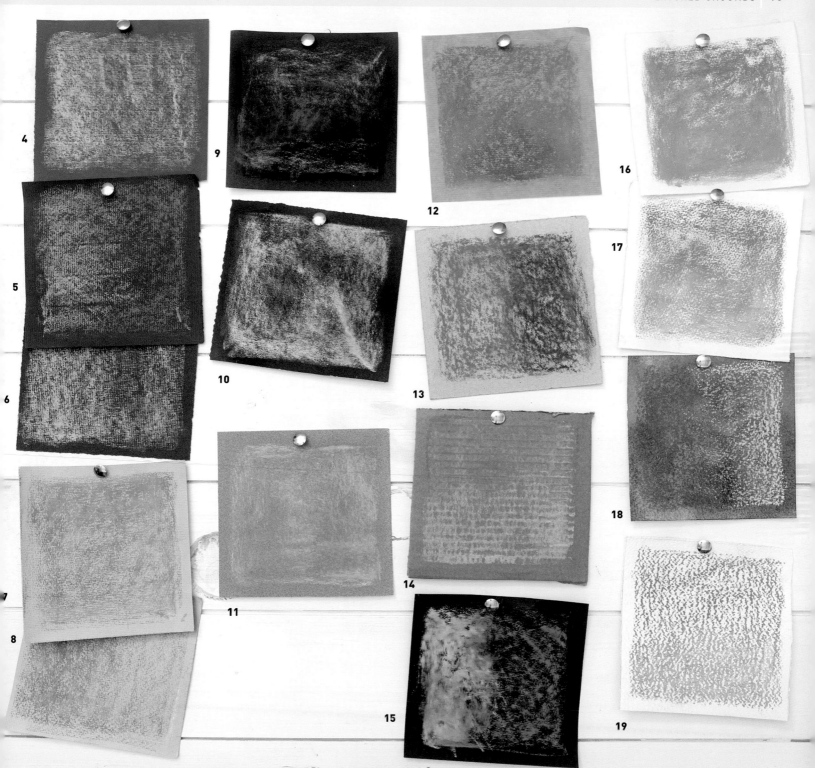

Gradations

This term refers to gradual transitions from one colour or tone to another. This is a vital element in modelling form and volume, particularly of curved or rounded forms, and in recreating certain effects of space, distance and atmosphere. Gradations of tone and colour may be very subtle and small-scale in figure work, portraiture and still life; while in landscape, colour transitions over large expanses of land, sky or water may be the key to capturing the sense of openness and the climatic mood.

Methods of conveying gradation vary from smooth effects of blending and shading to controlled textural variations formed by hatching and crosshatching or stippling. The simplest tonal gradation consists of laying a patch of fairly solid pastel colour and fading it gently outward with your fingers or a torchon. The same technique can be applied to merging two colours, fading them slightly where they overlap.

To create a smooth gradation when you are employing the basically linear character of a pastel stroke (as with shading and hatching) you need to consider whether you should overlay or alternate the colours at the point of transition, or introduce a third colour that links them together (yellow over red, for instance, or yellow-orange-red). You must avoid breaking the transition with a too-abrupt change, or overworking the transitional area excessively so that its texture stands out.

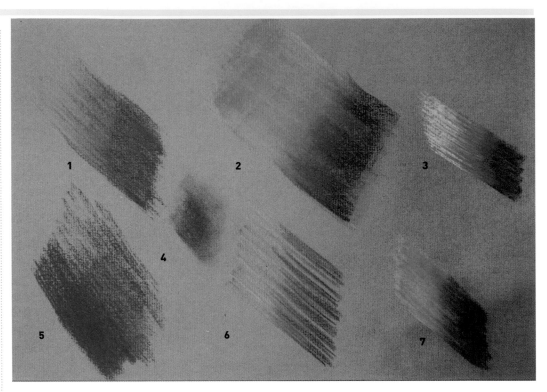

1 Gradation from one colour to another can also be achieved by shading, overlapping each colour on the previous one to integrate the hues.

2 The same principle of colour mixing is applied to yellow and red side strokes, blended with a torchon (see Blending, page 22) to produce the gradation through orange.

3 The moist texture of oil pastel creates a fusion of the graded colours. In this tonal gradation, the pink is an applied colour, not a mixture of the white and red.

4 An alternative way of producing graded tone is to use a torchon to spread the colour so that it fades outwards from the original marks.

5 To obtain a tonal gradation of one colour only, you can shade the pastel in close, even strokes, gradually lessening the pressure to lighten the tone.

6 This example of red grading into yellow is worked with hatched lines in the two main colours, which merge into orange where they meet and overlap.

7 In this example, the red and yellow colour bands are linked by a separate application of orange pastel at the centre.

Linear Marks

Any stroke that you apply using the tip or short edge of a pastel is basically linear in character, simply because the pastel's area of contact with the paper is confined. This does not mean your technique is limited, as you can use line work to build blends of tones and colours by systematic hatching and crosshatching, or by loose shading and scribbling. But there is also a wide variety of line qualities that you can exploit, in both structuring a drawing and developing the overall colour values. It is worth trying pastels of different shapes, sizes and textures to discover their full range.

Pastel is often thought of as an imprecise medium best suited to loose, impressionistic effects, but square-sectioned soft or hard pastels, and particularly pastel pencils, enable you to produce quite precise, sharp lines. A free stroke with a soft pastel produces a lightweight but thick, soft line; heavier pressure spreads the line and gives it more density. By varying pressure and by turning the pastel between your fingers, you can also produce fine lines that swell into grainy trails, or broad strokes tapering off narrowly. This range can be exploited in describing space, distance, volume and contour. It also contributes textural variety to hatched and crosshatched colour areas.

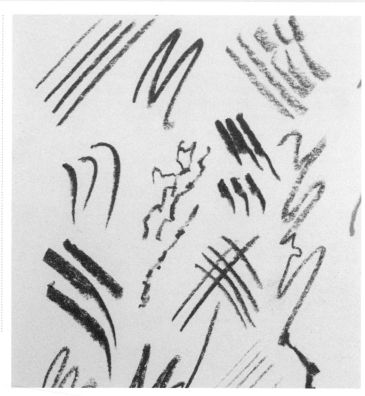

Soft pastel

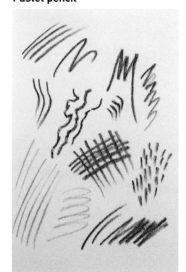

Pastel pencil

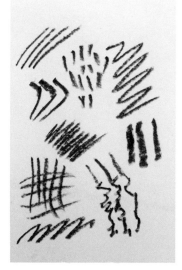

Oil pastel

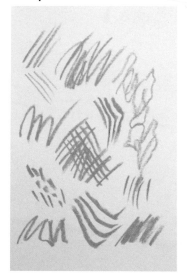

Hard pastel

Hatching and Crosshatching

As the classic method of creating tonal values using a linear medium, hatching is particularly associated with monochrome drawing techniques, but it can also be usefully applied to colour work. Hatching provides a means of varying effects of tone, colour and texture, and can enhance depth and form in a composition. Hatching consists of a series of roughly parallel lines, drawn close together. From a distance, the lines merge to give an impression of continuous tone or colour; from a closer view, the individual marks can be deciphered. The linear texture contributes a lively surface quality that can be a good alternative to, or contrast with, flat or blended colour.

Hatched lines need not be straight, nor uniform in thickness and density. They can be thick or thin, curved, tapered or broken, crisp or ragged (see also Linear Marks, page 17). You can use consistent strokes that follow the form they are describing, or vary the directions of strokes in adjacent areas of a drawing to suggest angled planes and contours in an object or spatial arrangement.

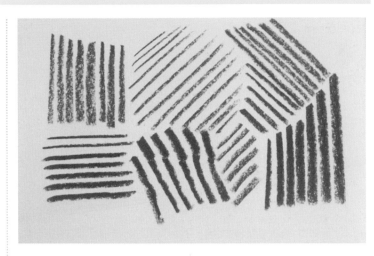

Variations of tone and texture can be obtained by varying the quality of the line between thick and thin, and the widths of the spaces between lines.

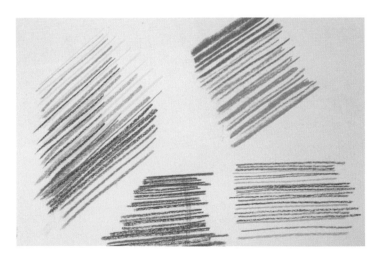

Colour variations, either mixed hues or gradations of colour, are developed by integrating two or more sets of lines made with different pastel sticks.

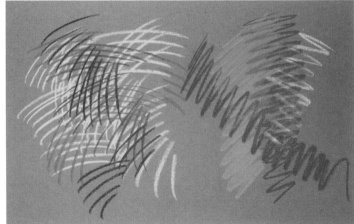

Hatched lines need not be straight or one-directional. Overlaid curves (left) build up a loose, informal kind of crosshatching. Scribbled marks are also effective when applied to a free style of imagery.

Crosshatching

In crosshatching you overlay one set of hatched lines on another, angled to produce a woven, mesh-like texture. As with hatching, the effects vary according to the line qualities and spaces between the lines, but because the texture is more complex, you can have a greater range of variation – different angles between two or more sets of lines; different colours for each succeeding layer.

When layering colours, use light but clean and decisive strokes to avoid devaluing hues and tones. Sometimes a little colour from an underlying layer is dragged into a fresh stroke, and this can have an enlivening effect that also helps to mesh the colours. Both hatching and crosshatching are useful techniques for keeping an active, open surface when you are working over previously laid pastel colour or on a coloured ground.

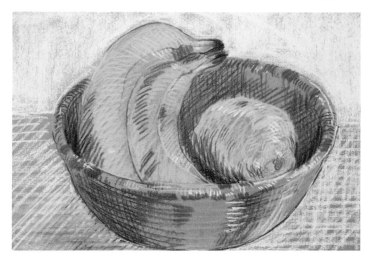

Traditionally, hatched lines follow the contours of the object. In this simple still life, the lines describe the curved shapes of the fruit and bowl, with straight lines emphasizing the flat plane of the tabletop. A limited range of colours is interwoven to create tonal variations, giving depth and form.

This detail shows how the extent and directions of the hatched lines are varied to indicate the different shapes of objects and the pattern of highlights and shadows.

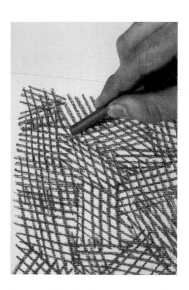

Crosshatched texture consists of two sets of lines roughly at right angles to each other, which may be in the same or different colours.

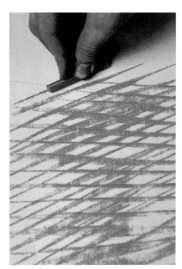

Using the long edge of a square-sectioned pastel stick produces a variable linear texture ranging from thin, sharp lines to broader, grainy marks.

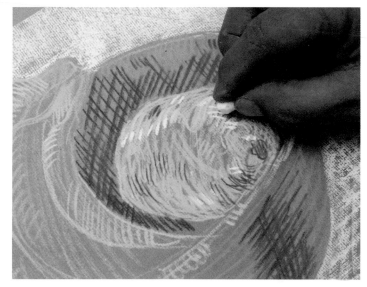

Shading

Shading is a way of applying continuous tone or colour. In monochrome drawing it is specifically associated with the process of modelling three-dimensional form through the effects of light and shade; in pastel work it applies to modulations of colour as well as tone.

The technique of shading is a controlled back-and-forth motion of the pastel travelling gradually across the working surface so that the strokes shade into one another. The effect is one of evenly massed colour rather than individual marks. Depending on the pressure you apply and the texture of the paper, the colour of the paper may modify that of the pastel, but not to the extent that it does in a linear shading method such as hatching (see page 18).

You can use shading to create areas of flat or graded colour, or as a basis for smooth blending of hues and tones. Conventionally, the effectiveness of shading depends upon working the strokes consistently in the same direction, which provides an even surface finish. However, when you are drawing a particular object, a change of direction in the shading can be used to indicate a change of direction in the object's surface, suggesting the planes or curves that describe its shape and volume.

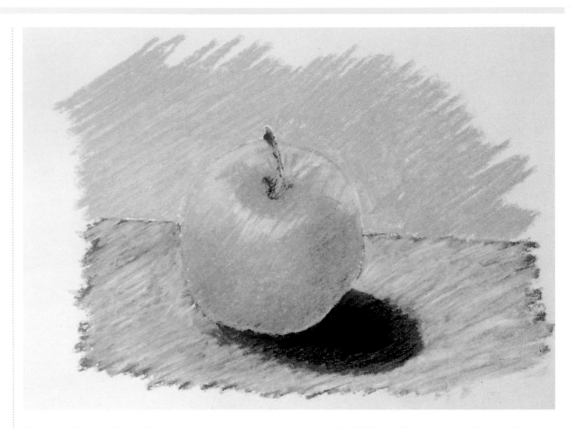

Heavy shading in soft pastel can create areas of flat, solid colour that give emphatic modelling to solid forms. Shade one colour into another to create highlights, shadows and subtle colour blends.

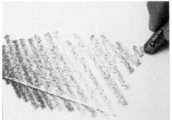

Oil pastel is used here, with a simple back and forth movement of the pastel tip. Varying the pressure enables you to develop tonal gradations. The texture of oil pastel generally creates an open, coarse texture, but you can build up layers of shaded colour for weight and intensity.

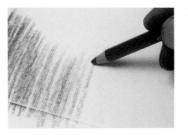

Pastel pencils are more gritty and fine-textured than pastel sticks, and the effect of shading is typically hard and linear. To give a clean edge to the shaded area, mask it off and take the pastel over the mask edge on each stroke.

Side Strokes

This is an important technique for building up broad colour areas with soft pastels, which is also effective with oil pastels. You simply draw the long side of a square- or round-sectioned pastel across the support to leave a broad band of grainy colour. The depth of tone or colour depends upon the pressure you apply and the texture of the support. A heavily toothed surface will not completely fill with colour even if you apply strong pressure, and the amount of colour showing through from the support modifies the effect of the pastel pigment.

You can juxtapose side strokes edge-to-edge to block in large areas of colour (see Blocking In, page 23). You can overlay them, working in the same direction or opposing directions in successive layers, to develop subtle colour blends and mixtures. The grainy texture of a side stroke can be left as it is, or with soft pastel you can use a torchon or your fingers to blend the colour more smoothly.

Do not overlay side strokes too heavily or in too many layers, or the colours will become overmixed and degraded.

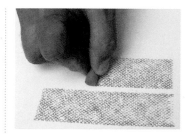

To lay the colour evenly, draw the side of the pastel stick firmly across the paper surface. The density of the colour depends on the pressure you apply and the quality of the paper grain.

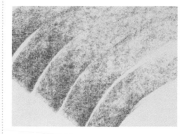

You can obtain graded colour effects by lightening the pressure as you extend the stroke.

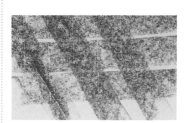

Side strokes can be overlaid in different directions to produce a very broad, grainy form of crosshatching or to build up colour density. Colour mixes can be made by overlaying different colours in this way.

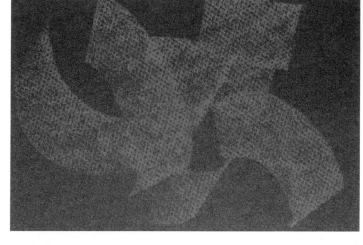

As with linear marks made with the tip of the pastel, side strokes will reflect the rapid movement of your hand. Lively, curved, short strokes build up an active texture.

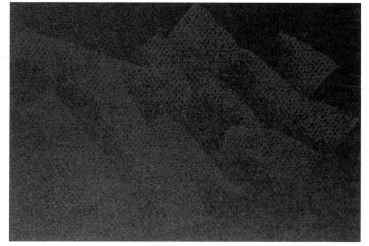

To produce a more varied, broken stroke, angle the pastel very slightly to apply more pressure on one end than on the other.

Blending

In traditional methods of pastel painting, particularly as applied to portraiture, colours were smoothed and blended together to produce images with a high degree of surface finish comparable to the effects of contemporary oil painting techniques. To the modern eye, much of the medium's impact comes from the grainy, rough textures of pastel and loose networks of individual pastel strokes. But the subtleties of blended colours and smooth gradation of hues and tones are vital elements in rendering specific materials and surface qualities – soft fabrics, for instance, or uniform, reflective surfaces such as metal and glass – and atmospheric impressions. Blended colours also provide visual contrast when integrated with loose pastel strokes and broken colour in a composition.

The special tool for blending soft pastels is a torchon – a tight roll of paper that is shaped like a pencil and used in the same way – you "shade" into the pastel strokes with the tip or side of the torchon to spread and blend the powdery colour. You obtain a clean point on the torchon by unwinding some of the paper from the tip. A torchon enables you to control the blending quite precisely, and is thus ideal for small areas. Alternatively, you can use your fingers, a cotton bud, tissues or a rag, or a brush (soft-textured fabrics and brushes will lift some of the colour).

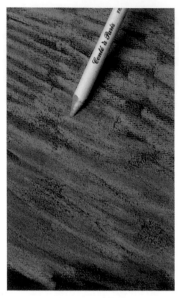

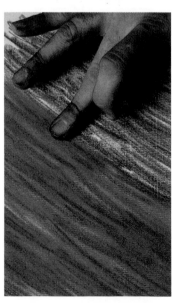

Blending with a torchon
Lay down the pastel colour and gently rub the surface with the tip or side of the torchon to soften and blend the colours.

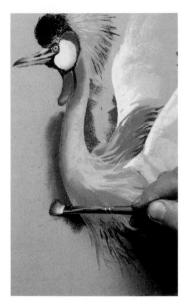

Blending with a brush
Use a short hog-hair or synthetic bristle brush to break down the grain of the pastel particles and spread the colour evenly.

Blending with fingers
Rubbing with your finger merges the colours and presses the pastel dust into the paper grain. It is an effective way of blending linear or side strokes in soft pastel.

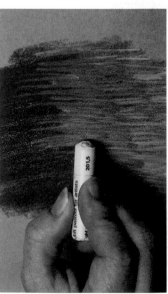

Blended strokes
With oil pastels and hard pastels, which do not spread so smoothly on the surface of the paper, use short strokes to overlay one colour on another, varying the pressure so that the integrated marks produce an impression of mixed hues and tones.

Blocking In

This term refers to the process of rapidly laying in the main shapes and broad colour areas of a composition before starting to develop the detail. The purpose is to provide yourself with a basic structure for the painting and a tonal or colour key relating to the overall impression of the subject.

The quickest way to block in large colour areas is using side strokes (see page 21) to apply broad patches of grainy colour, but you can use any method of shading with the tip or edge of the pastel stick. However, this is a preliminary stage of your work, and it is important not to overwork the pastel or you will encounter problems in keeping the colours clean and strokes distinct when you start to build up the detail. Whatever method you use to block in basic shapes, tones and colours, use minimal pressure so that these initial layers are lightweight and open-textured.

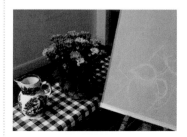

1 A quick outline sketch of the subject establishes the main shapes as a guideline for laying in the colour areas.

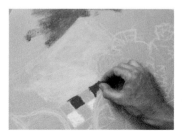

2 Working with one colour at a time, the artist starts to fill each area with a loose, open layer of pastel. When blocking in, use the side or tip of the pastel to apply the colour freely.

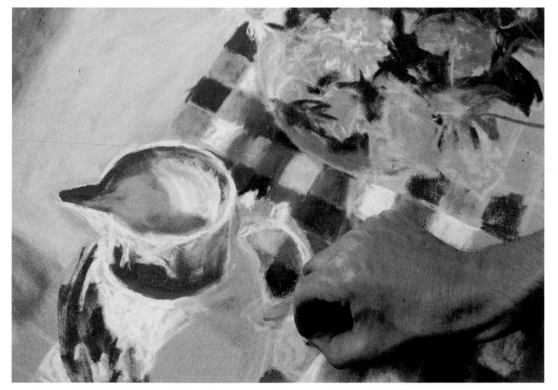

3 Complex forms like flowers and foliage can be blocked in initially as simple shapes with a suggestion of colour and texture, bearing in mind that this sort of detail can be developed and reworked at a later stage.

4 The artist gradually works his way around the whole image to achieve a broad impression of all elements of the subject. Notice how the still life has clearly taken on a sense of solid form, although the shapes are as yet imprecise and the pastel marks are still free and vigorous.

Broken Colour

Pastel is an ideal medium for achieving broken-colour effects – the shape and size of the pastel stick and the small-scale gestures your hand makes when manipulating it provide the basic elements of this technique.

As the term suggests, broken colour is the complete opposite of flat or smoothly blended colour. You build whole colour areas using short strokes of the pastel, juxtaposing or interweaving two or more colours. This enables you to produce rough blends and colour mixes, one hue or tone modifying another. From the appropriate viewing distance, broken colour "reads" as a coherent surface effect; from a closer view, you can appreciate the colour interactions and lively textural qualities of the mingled strokes.

As with any colour medium, overmixing devalues the contribution of all the component colours and results in a muddy effect, so you need to think carefully about the range and number of individual colours that you use. You might use three kinds of blue, for example, to create the impression of a very vibrant, active, single colour, or employ a tonal range that enables you to suggest light and shade. You may wish to combine harmonious colours for a gentle effect, or introduce contrasts to intensify strong passages – massed foliage in a landscape, for instance, could be represented with a serene combination of yellow, green and blue, or you could create depth and warmth by juxtaposing greens with red, orange, brown or purple.

One of the colour elements may be supplied by the colour of the support, which also gives an underlying unity to the mass of pastel strokes. A white or light-tinted ground contributes luminosity, a dark-toned support enhances the brilliance of applied hues.

This technique works well with all types of pastels, the shape and texture of the particular medium governing the delicacy or coarseness of the broken colour effect.

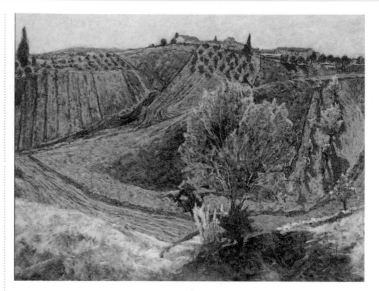

◄ **PATRICK CULLEN**
PURPLE FIELDS NEAR CENTALDO
In this landscape, each area is interpreted as a complex mass of broken colour, consisting of interwoven and overlaid marks. Careful integration of the colour values gives a coherent structure to the overall view and its individual elements.

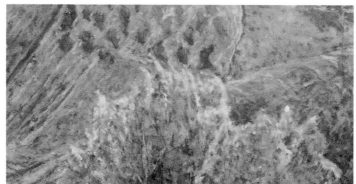

Detail of centre: The range of closely related colours applied to the tree foliage implies both its mass and detail, the brighter hues drawing out the shape from the background of more muted colour.

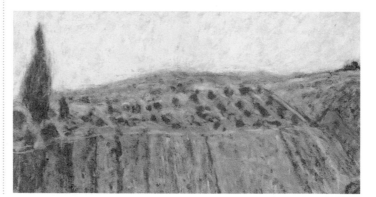

Detail of top left: The colour variation in the grassy and ploughed fields is naturally suggested by their individual forms and textures, but note how the open sky is also treated as a mass of overlaid, pale tones, not as a single flat colour.

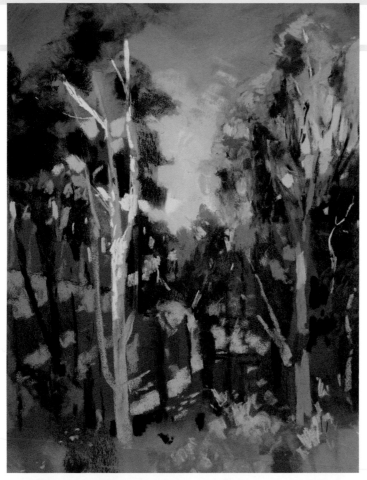

◀ MARGARET LARLHAM
EUCALYPTUS GROVE
Warm pinks and mauves are juxtaposed with olive greens and dark neutrals, creating a vibrant interplay of colours and shapes that beautifully captures the character of the tall eucalyptus trees.

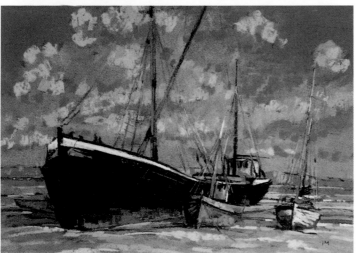

◀ GEOFF MARSTERS
BARGE, THE RAYBEL
In this picture the pastel strokes are used more emphatically to construct the varied shapes and surface values. The vibrant colour combinations are boldly stated, but carefully arranged to develop the impression of form and space.

Building Up

Unless you are using pastels only for quick sketches, or working in line alone, you will need to develop your own strategies for building up colour effects and detail. Pastel is a medium that demands a gradual approach if you are to avoid overworking the surface too quickly, or losing the clarity of colour and detail through too much mixing of marks and textures. Many people find it easiest to control the very loose texture of soft pastels by fixing the surface at regular intervals as the work progresses, and this suggests an approach that involves "staging" the colour applications.

One common method of building up a pastel painting is to begin by blocking in broad colour areas quickly, then applying a range of techniques to develop form, detail and texture. If you are rapidly laying in an initial impression of tones and colours overall, keep the layers of colour light and grainy so that you do not fill the tooth of the paper too quickly and arrive too soon at a "solid" surface quality that resists further colour applications.

Most artists agree that the best approach to building up a composition is to work all areas of the image to the same level of surface quality and visual detail at each stage, before moving on to more complex or intricate elements. If you complete one particular area of a painting in full detail before applying yourself to the next, it is difficult to achieve an image that has balance and consistency. As pastel is such a direct medium, which forces you to make immediate decisions on tonal and colour values, you need to be constantly aware of the interaction of different elements of the image and how, for instance, introducing a new colour may give an unexpected cast to the colours you have already applied.

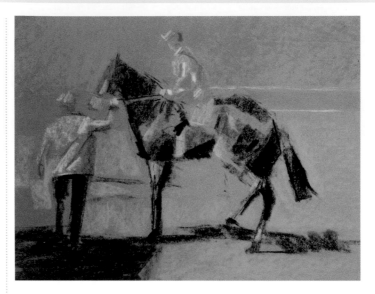

Soft pastel
1 The whole image is first blocked in rapidly (see Blocking In, page 23), using side strokes and sketchy lines to lay out the main colour areas and individual forms of horse, jockey and trainer.

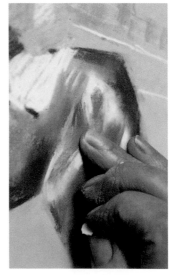

2 Each section of the image is built up with thicker layers of colour, using a combination of hues and tones to develop the modelling of the forms. The specific texture of the horse's glossy coat is imitated by finger-blending the pastel marks.

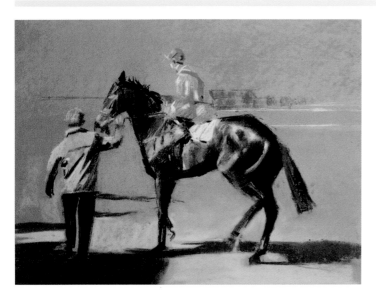

3 As this treatment is applied to increasing areas of the image, the picture gains form and structure. Strong lights and shadows in the foreground enhance the spatial qualities.

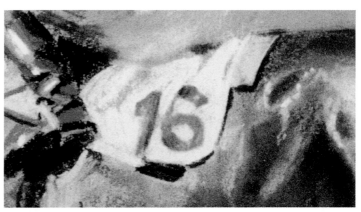

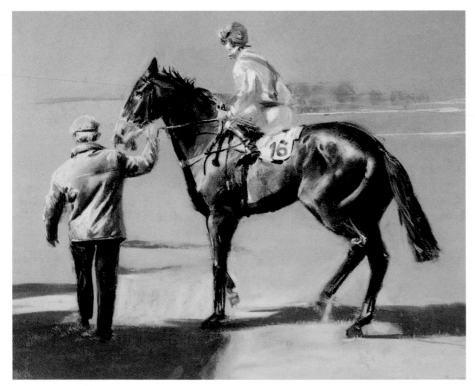

4, 5 In the finished image, each form has been fully modelled with a subtly varied range of tones and hues. Careful blending has been used to describe the weight, solidity and surface textures of the horse and figures, but there is still enough evidence of the individual pastel marks to give the image a lively rhythm and suggestion of movement appropriate to the subject. The detail (above) shows how features such as the saddle and harness and the jockey's clothing are drawn with a more complex network of individual marks and small patches of colour. Tonal contrasts, as in the folds of the boots and saddlecloth and the dark cast shadows beneath them, are boldly emphasized.

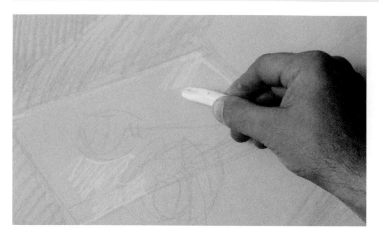

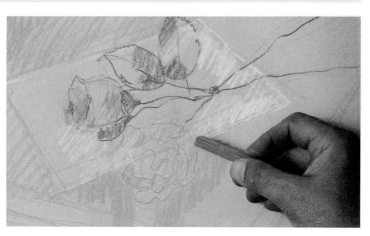

Hard pastel

1 The composition is first blocked in as a monochrome sketch, using grey and white pastels to outline and loosely shade in the basic shapes.

2 The colours of the leaves and flowers are described with light and mid-toned hues. Linear techniques such as shading and hatching are used to put in the blocks of colour.

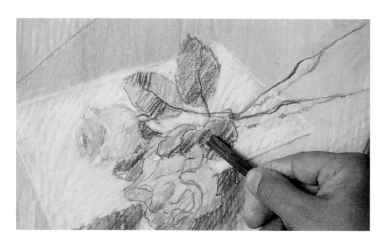

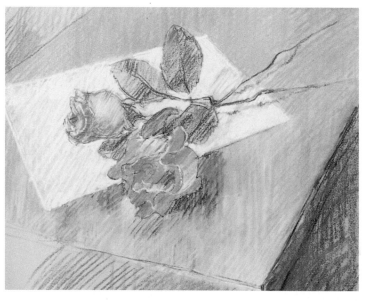

3 Colour detail is gradually developed, introducing additional hues to describe the variation of the flower petals, and dark tones to model the shadow areas. In places, the linear marks are lightly rubbed with a finger to spread and soften the colour.

4 The same techniques are used to build up the image in layers, reworking different parts of the picture in stages. The dense pastel marks merge into an increasingly detailed impression of form and surface texture.

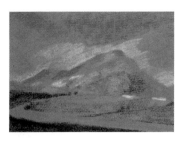

Oil pastel

1 In the blocking stage, the main colour areas of the landscape are established using side strokes and loose shading.

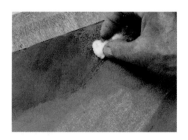

2 To blend the sky colours, a little turpentine is applied to a cotton ball and rubbed over the pastel, softening the colour and texture.

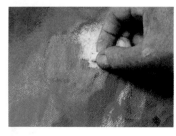

3 The range of tone and colour is built up by overlaying the oil pastel more thickly. This process of layering and blending the colours is applied to the image overall.

4 The silhouettes of trees in the foreground and middle distance are painted with a brush. This is done by picking up the colour from the tip of a pastel stick on a brush moistened with turpentine, then transferring the colour to the working surface.

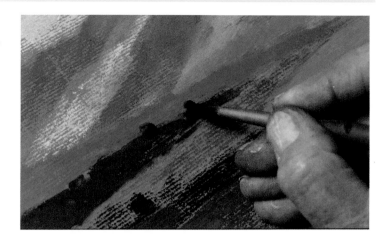

5 As the main forms and colour areas emerge in more detail, pale tints are overlaid. The tip of the pastel stick is used to apply highlights on the road, grass and hillside, enhancing the impression of light and space. Note the variations in the density of the pastel layers, so that in places the paper colour shows through, giving textural contrast against the more solid pastel colour.

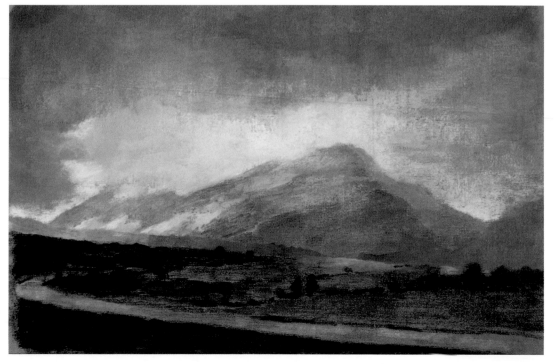

Scumbling

This is an adaptation of a traditional oil painting technique, in which a thin veil of colour is applied to modify underlying layers. In painting, you use a light, scrubbing motion of the brush. The comparable effect with pastels is achieved using light, circular strokes loosely rubbed over the paper tooth, to deposit a fine layer of textured pigment without either obliterating or picking up the previously laid colour. The side or blunted tip of the pastel can be used.

The hazy effect of scumbling can be exploited working light over dark, to create a slight shimmer and enhance the colours' luminosity, or by laying dark colour over a pale or vivid hue, to subtly "knock back" the original colour and give depth to the image. If you combine close-toned colours, they will mix optically to give the impression of a "hybrid" colour that has a more active surface effect than smooth colour blending but a more delicate texture than typical broken colour effects.

The technique is best suited to soft pastels, but with a careful, light touch you can obtain good scumbling effects with oil pastel also.

Soft pastel
In this example, light-toned colour is applied with gentle circular strokes of the pastel tip over an even spread of grainy mid-toned orange.

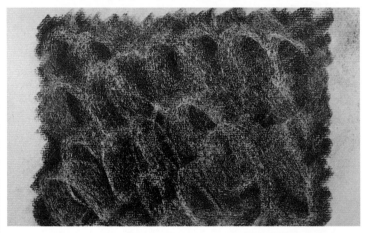

Soft pastel
This more rhythmic, open texture was achieved by applying a short length of pastel in looping side strokes over the heavily shaded brown base layer.

Oil pastel
This example shows the effect of two light-toned oil pastels scumbled onto dark red pastel paper. The pink was applied first, then the blue, in both cases using the flattened tip of the pastel stick.

Overlaying Colours

The build-up of layer upon layer of colours is the great fascination of pastel work, from broad drifts of loose colour laying out the basic shapes to the small accents and highlights that add the finishing touches.

The textures of the medium and support allow glints of colour to show through in successive applications. When you overlay open-textured side strokes or soft scumbling or apply linear or broken colour effects such as crosshatching, feathering and stipplingover flat colour, you can obtain subtle or brilliant colour mixes and modifications that on close inspection show their interwoven marks as individual hues. Even a thick impasto stroke dragged across an area of previously laid colour may have ragged edges that reveal fragments of the underlying hue.

These effects are best seen in soft pastel rendering, where the wide colour range and textural versatility of the medium can be given free rein. So that the layering processes retain the richness of the contributing colours, it is advisable to apply a light spray of fixative at various stages of the work.

▼ MARGARET LARLHAM
BEND IN THE RUAHA RIVER WITH HIDDEN MONKEYS
Overlaid colours are obvious throughout this scene – particularly in the river, where purples of various hues have been softly blended with the underlying blues to create a lovely impression of light and shade on the water, and on the foreground rocks, where dragging the side of the pastel very lightly over the paper has allowed some of the paper texture to show through.

▼ ROY SPARKES
FRINDSBURY GARDEN, ELIZABETH H
The slight translucency of oil pastel is exploited here, forming interesting textural contrasts between areas of thin, almost flat colour and the layered effect of successive applications, using short stabbing strokes and circular motions to overlay and interweave the varied hues.

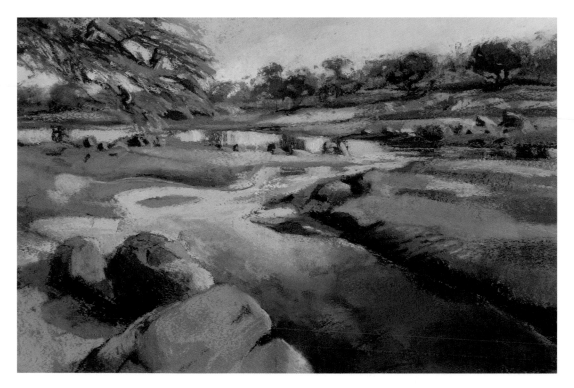

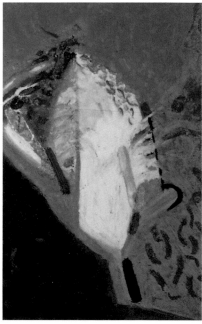

Edge Qualities

Different subjects require different treatments in terms of conveying solid shapes and forms and qualities of light, mood and atmosphere. To take a simple example, man-made environments and objects frequently incorporate hard edges, well-defined contours and sharply angled shadows, whereas natural subjects may have more complex and amorphous forms, or curved and fluid shapes, and subtle modulations of light and shade. The ways in which you define the edges and contours of your colour areas can help to give your rendering detail and precision.

Soft-edge qualities are achieved by using open-textured side strokes, by letting massed linear strokes create a fuzzy or irregular contour, or by gently rubbing the edge of a colour area with your fingers or a torchon to fade it indistinctly. Hard edges are achieved by highly controlled shading of dense colour, by giving a definite outline to a shape – which could be in a slightly lighter or darker tone than the main colour area – or by using masking techniques to isolate the required shape (see page 66).

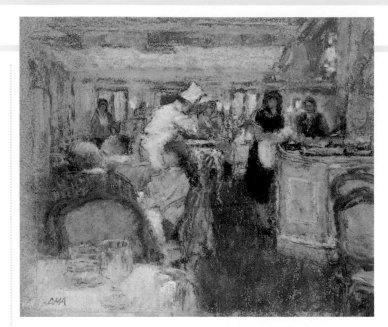

◀ **DIANA ARMFIELD**
LUNCH AT FORTNUM'S
In this interior view in soft pastel, all the edge qualities are quite free, giving the image an expressive, gentle atmosphere. The architectural structure and furnishings of the restaurant are described with a variety of thick and thin linear strokes and grainy patches of overlaid colour. The techniques are fully integrated throughout the image, but there is a subtle emphasis on solid, static forms such as the bar counter and chairs.

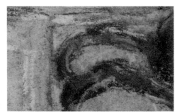

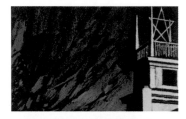

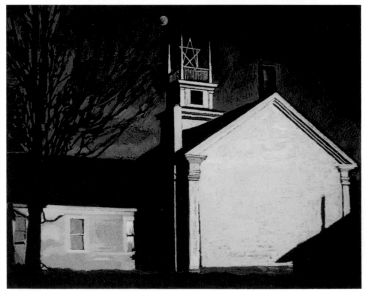

◀ **JOHN ELLIOT**
NORMAN ROCKWELL'S CHURCH
The oil pastel has been applied in controlled areas of shading on a dark ground. The edge qualities in the building are crisp and hard, with the direction of the pastel strokes following the outlines of the forms. The organic quality of the tree branches is shown in ragged edges emerging from the looser treatment of the sky colours that form their background.

Accenting

Colour accents are the little touches of colour you use to "lift" a work in pastel. They add emphasis and points of focus in a composition. The marks you make may be brief and quite abstract in themselves, but they should derive from something that you see in your subject which, accurately translated onto the page, enhances the definition and detail of your drawing.

Accenting can be similar to highlighting (see page 34) – like the tiny points of pure white or very pale tints that give life to flesh tones and facial features in a portrait. But colour accents apply more broadly to overall colour effects, relating to local colours, lights and shadows. Because an accent is a small mark, you can be surprisingly bold with its colour value and still find that it works effectively in relation to the surrounding colour areas – a patch of strong violet giving richness to a dark cast shadow, for example, or a streak of brilliant pink lighting the far horizon in a landscape.

The kind of marks you put down in accenting relate to the subject and may be interpreted as lines, dots, dashes, brief scribbles or small, irregular shapes.

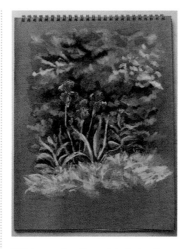

1 This small soft-pastel study of flowers and foliage is nearing completion. The natural variation in the flower colours provides bright colour accents, but the foliage background lacks depth and detail.

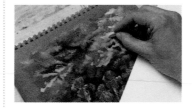

2 At the top right-hand corner of the image, touches of pale blue and yellow are put in to indicate glimpses of sky and sunlight reflecting on the leaves.

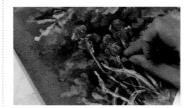

3 The shadow areas behind the flowers are strengthened, using warm brown over black to contrast with the greens and yellows.

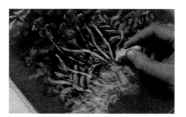

4 The lighter green grasses in the foreground area are retouched with a pale mauve pastel to give cool colour contrast against the warm shadows.

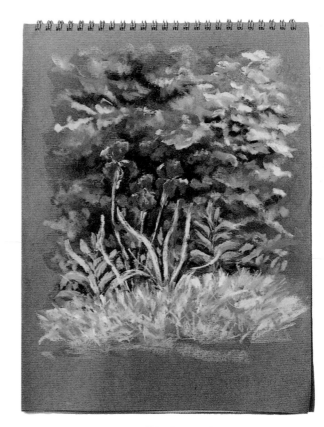

5 In the completed image, the colour accents give more definition to the form and texture of the leaf masses and enhance the sense of depth between foreground and background elements.

Highlighting

Highlights represent the points of light most intensely reflected from the surface of an object, and they add sparkle and a high finish to a pastel rendering. Highlighting is usually done in the final stages, as this enables you to judge the highest tones against the other colours and prevents dirtying the whites with subsequent colour applications. Highlights can either be added with quick, decisive touches of the pastel stick, or you can use an eraser to reclaim the white of the paper. The latter method will only be successful if the quality of the pastel marks is such that you can lift the colour cleanly – you will not get an effective highlight if the pigment is firmly impressed into the paper grain.

Applied highlights are usually more effective, and you will quickly acquire the dexterity to overlay a crisp, white mark without smearing or picking up the underlying colour. If the colour layers are thickly built up, you can scrape out gently with a razor or scalpel blade and apply a light spray of fixative before adding the lights.

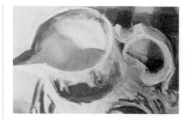

1 Smooth-textured materials such as ceramics, glass and metal throw off the most intense highlights. In this ceramic jug, lit from the left-hand side, the lip, rim and handle need to be strongly highlighted.

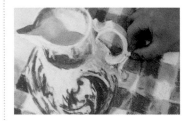

2 Additional highlighting follows the modelling of the form; pure white pastel is thickly applied to enhance the lit effect on the outer curve of the jug handle.

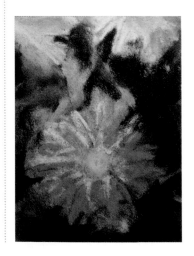

3 Soft-textured forms such as flower petals do not reflect light so strongly, but need gentle highlighting to emphasize the petal shapes. Notice that the artist has used lighter strokes for this effect to maintain textural contrast.

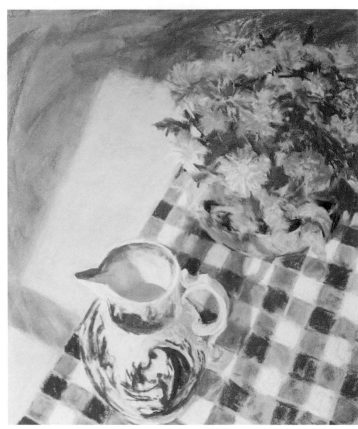

4 In the finished image, the overall pattern of light and shade is clearly described and the highlighting gives extra definition to the individual forms of the jug and flowers.

Tinting

Like highlighting (opposite), tinting is a way of heightening the contrasts of light and shade in a rendering. If you find that a portrait painting, for example, seems a little flat and lifeless when it is nearing completion, you may need to enhance the paler tones and colours to give a soft sheen or bloom to certain areas of the image. Similarly, it may help in conveying both the form and texture of fabric folds – silk or velvet, for instance. The effect need not be as strong or distinct as a true highlight; the idea is just to "lift" the colour values.

You may find that fine linear strokes overlaid on the colour area are effective, from a distance giving an optical effect of the required tone and enlivening the surface from a closer viewpoint. However, you may wish to blend the tint subtly, picking up the colour from the previous layer – for this you can use a torchon or your finger to stroke the pastel particles together.

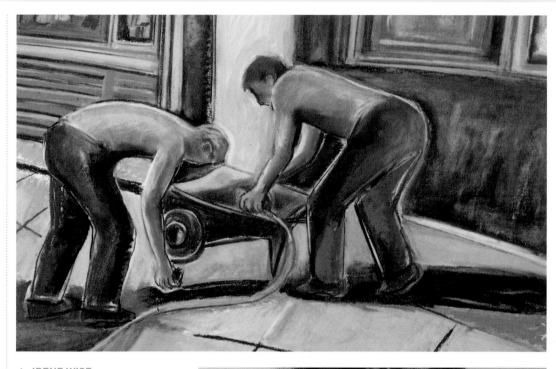

▲ **IRENE WISE**
ROAD DIGGERS
The qualities of light and shade are enhanced in various interesting ways in this stylized composition. In the yellow door that frames the head of the right-hand figure, the pure hue is loosely blended with a paler tint. On the bodies, linear marks are applied over rubbed and blended colour. Complementary contrast is introduced in the intense, bright blue shaded over brown on the legs; colour variation can be as effective as tonal contrast in giving impact to the modelling of forms.

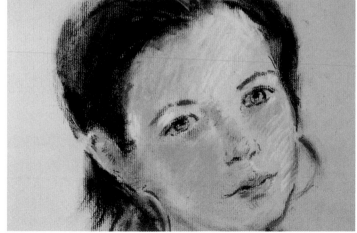

The angle of the light falling on the subject's face is delicately conveyed with loosely hatched strokes of pale flesh tint, rather than with smoothly blended colour. The base tone of the skin is formed by the paper colour.

Dry Wash

This technique strictly applies only to soft pastels, as the true effect of a dry wash depends upon the powdery quality of pastels made with a minimum of binding material. To begin with, you reduce the pastel stick to powder by scraping the long edge with a knife blade. Hold it over a palette, dish or piece of clean paper, to catch the powder as it falls, and try to graze, not chip, the edge of the pastel with the blade, so that the powdered colour is quite fine.

When you have a reasonable quantity of powdered colour, use a rag, fine sponge or cotton ball to pick up the powder and spread it on the paper, working evenly across the support to lay down a flat colour tint. To produce tonal or colour gradations, you can strengthen the colour in selected areas, or overlay additional colours.

This is one method of creating a coloured ground for pastel work, using colours and textures that will be naturally sympathetic to the pastel strokes you overlay. It is also a good way of developing hazy or atmospheric effects in landscape rendering – representing large areas of sky, land or water, for example.

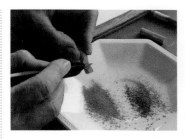

1 Use a craft-knife blade or similar tool to scrape the edge of the pastel stick evenly, collecting a heap of fine-textured powder colour.

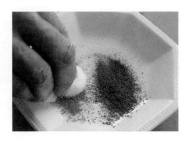

2 If you are using more than one colour, these can be mixed and blended on the paper surface. Dab a cotton ball into the first colour to pick up some of the powder.

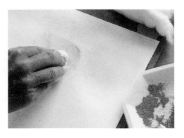

3 Rub the cotton ball across the paper surface, laying down a thin, even colour tint. Work it well into the paper grain and increase the tonal depth gradually with successive applications.

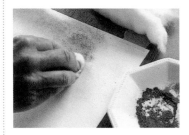

4 Apply the second colour in the same way, working it into the required areas of the paper. Varying the pressure you apply to the cotton ball creates subtle differences of tone and texture.

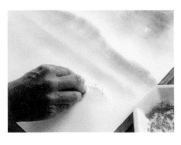

5 To apply a third or subsequent colour, simply repeat the process as required. Keep the batches of powder separate to avoid devaluing the colours.

6 As with this example, you can use the dry wash technique to block in the basic colour areas of a composition, or you can simply use it as a method of tinting the paper to create an overall colour key.

Feathering

The term "feathering" accurately represents the technique – quick, light, linear strokes made with the tip of the pastel, keeping the direction of the strokes consistent. Feathering is a way of overlaying one colour on another to modify the original hue or tone, or of integrating a range of hues to form a coherent but active surface effect of blended and mixed colours.

Because feathering is formed of a mass of individual strokes, it is a good way of adding richness to a colour area that seems dull or flat, particularly where you have already applied solid or blended colour that has filled the paper tooth and you need to revive the liveliness of your drawing's texture. As a modifier, feathering provides the opportunity to produce subtle changes of colour character – to lighten or darken a mid-tone that lacks contrast with surrounding colours, for instance; to "cool" a warm colour, or vice versa; to enliven hues that have deadened by introducing light touches of a contrasting colour.

This is a particularly useful technique for developing mixed colours with hard pastels and pastel pencils, which do not blend as easily as soft pastels. Also, because you must use a light touch, you can achieve successful feathering with oil pastels without ending up with a smeary, unworkable surface.

This area of blended hues is built up on the white ground of the paper by overlaying light, quick strokes of pink, purple and pale blue.

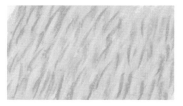

The same colours are used here on a flat ground of yellow pastel. Each successive colour application modifies the effect of individual hues.

Very fine, elongated strokes are used here to produce a shimmering effect of colour and texture composed of light-toned hues.

▼ GEOFF MARSTERS
IHI AT ALDEBURGH
Feathering is used very effectively here to enhance the atmospheric qualities of the image and create subtly vibrant colour mixes.

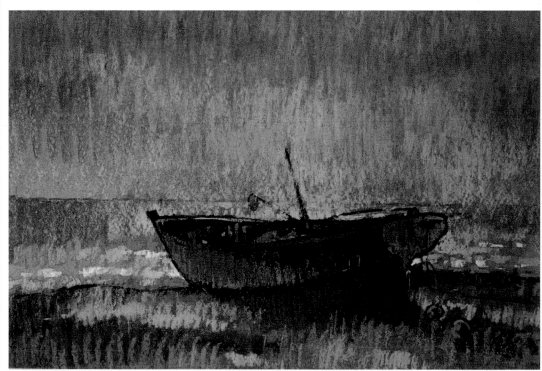

Impasto

In painting, this term refers to thick strokes of colour, applied with a brush or knife, that stand out from the surface of the canvas or board. Applied to pastel, it means using heavy, thick strokes of a soft pastel or oil pastel that deposit the full strength of its colour and texture on the working surface.

You can lay impasto strokes directly on the surface or build them up over thinner, grainy colour. The facility for overworking is ultimately limited, because with this technique the tooth of the paper fills more quickly and the surface soon becomes resistant to further applications.

Edgar Degas (1834–1917) achieved wonderfully rich, thick textural effects, often by unorthodox means. He would sometimes work dry colour into a wet vehicle, experimenting with oils, varnishes and fixatives, so that the pastel colour became a kind of workable paste – a true impasto medium.

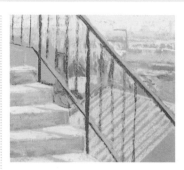

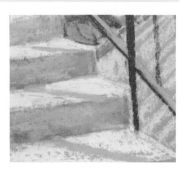

Soft pastel
1 The townscape view is blocked in quickly using heavy, free strokes to establish overall colour values. In the areas where colours have been overlaid, you can see already the rich texture of the thickly worked strokes.

2 The increasing density of the pastel layers is evident with the gradual disappearance of the paper colour, now virtually eliminated from the image except where faint traces have been left to stand as mid-tones and light shadowing; for instance, on the risers of the steps and the façade of the building on the right.

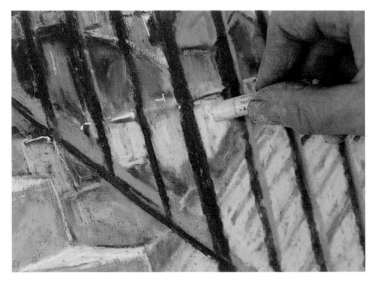

3 Thick impasto strokes in pale tones produce very intense highlighting. Surface texture becomes very rich, with broken colour where strokes are overlaid and ragged, grainy edge qualities.

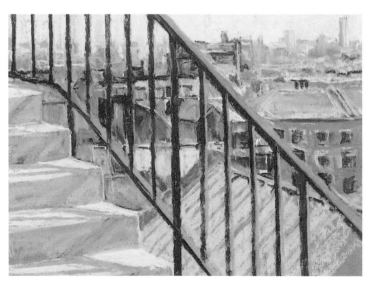

4 The finished image is similar to a brush painting in oil or gouache, with a cohesive, opaque surface. But working this way with pastels, you have very direct control of the individual marks and colour mixes.

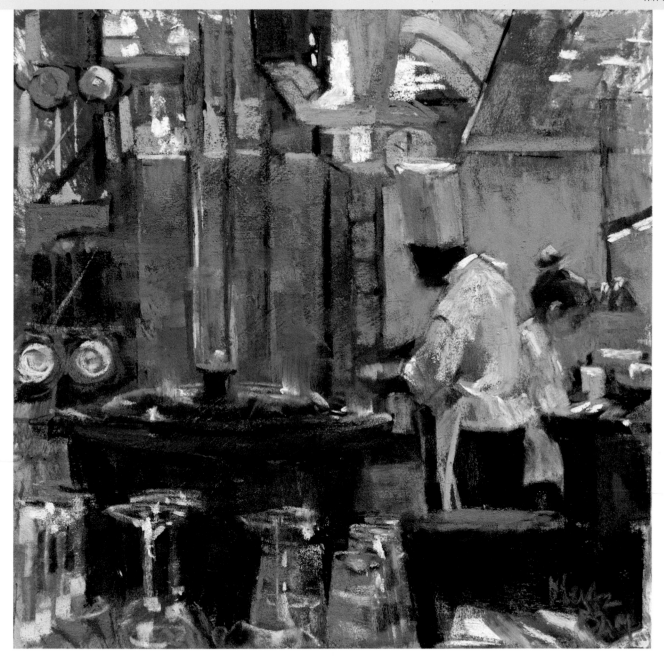

▲ NANCIE KING MERTZ
BEECHER'S CHEESE
In this atmospheric piece that the artist created from a photo she took
through a NYC shop window, thick layers of pigment are used, especially
on the highlights. The effect is to make these areas really sparkle.

Scraping Out

This is a technique that enables you to re-establish a workable surface when you have built up layers of soft pastel very thickly and find it difficult to apply further colour. A heavy accumulation of pigment particles can be scraped back with the flat edge of a fine blade, such as a scalpel or craft-knife blade. You can then spray the area lightly with fixative and redraw when the fixative has dried.

Some artists use the technique very successfully as a positive drawing element. Scraping out pastel layers has the effect of fusing the colours in a rough, scratchy overall texture; if a coloured ground is used, its underlying shade also becomes meshed into the pastel colour. The texture typically has a linear quality corresponding to the direction in which the blade travels over the surface, which gives additionally a sense of movement.

You have to manipulate the blade carefully, to avoid shaving the grain of the paper or digging into the surface. Because of the textural interaction of the medium and support in pastel work, it is very difficult to either disguise or accommodate actual surface damage.

Linear texture

Scraping out can be used as a positive element of drawing technique for introducing very fine linear texture in a colour composition. In this example, the tip of a blade has been used to draw into heavily applied colour, creating the whiskery effect of the seedheads and enhancing the complexity of the varied directional lines in the massed grasses.

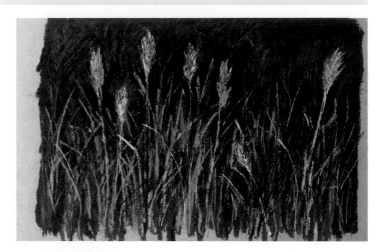

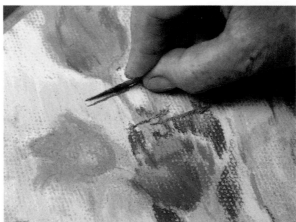

1 In an area of the composition that is to be reworked, the colour is scraped back using the flat edge of a lightweight craft-knife blade. To avoid damaging the surface, follow the grain of the pastel marks.

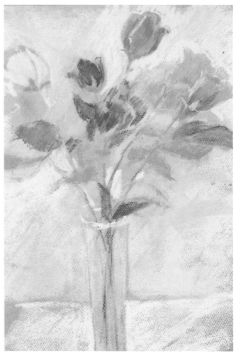

2 In reapplying pastel colour over the scraped section, the marks are built up with the same consistency and direction as in the surrounding areas.

Sgraffito

The term sgraffito derives from the Italian word meaning "scratched", and the technique involves working into layered colours with a sharp tool, scratching into the top layer to reveal another colour underneath. To do this successfully, you need a medium with sufficient body to create a clean effect when scratched into – soft pastels or oil pastels that can be thickly laid – and you must be methodical about preparing the colour layers to achieve the effect you want.

The basic method involves covering the support with a layer of solid colour well rubbed into the paper grain, then applying a second, quite heavy layer of another colour on top, but this time without rubbing it in. If you use soft pastel, fix the first colour before working over it. You can then scratch into the top layer with a fine scalpel blade or stylus.

Variations include working dark over light or light over dark, using more than one colour in either layer; applying a textured rather than flat top layer; and applying pastel over a coloured ground of ink or paint, rather than over a previous application of pastel.

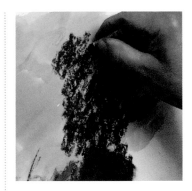

Oil pastel over watercolour

1 The base colour is painted with a loose wash of yellow-green watercolour. When this is dry, black oil pastel is shaded thickly over the surface and rubbed to produce a smoothly blended texture.

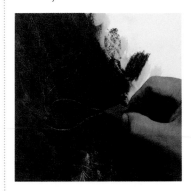

2 The drawing is begun with the tip of a craft-knife blade, taking care just to scratch back the oil pastel colour and avoid digging into the paper surface.

3 This example is worked as a line drawing, using closely hatched lines to produce the impression of variations of colour and tone.

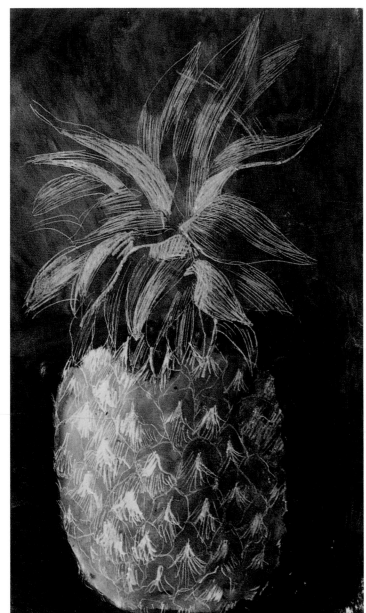

Erasures

It becomes progressively more difficult to erase pastel as you build up the colour layers. Any method that you use for erasure interferes with the natural texture of the pastel strokes and can also spoil the paper surface. In other words, do not count on making major changes in this way beyond the early stages of a pastel rendering. As long as the pastel has not completely filled the paper grain, in later stages you should still be able to make corrections by overworking the part you want to change.

While the pastel is still thinly applied and fairly loose on the surface, you can use a hog-hair or synthetic bristle brush to flick away the powdery colour. The best type of commercially made eraser for pastels is a kneaded eraser – it has a slightly tacky consistency that picks up the loose pastel without the need to rub the surface heavily, which can smear the colour or flatten the paper grain. A plastic eraser is useful for cleaning off the colour dust that accumulates around individual shapes and at the edges of a composition; carefully manipulated, it can also be used to erase thinly applied colour and retrieve highlight areas. Heavy pigment particles can be scraped away with a single-sided razor blade or lightweight, sharp knife blade, and you can then follow up with a kneaded eraser.

Many pastellists recommend fresh bread as the only medium for erasing soft pastel. A small piece gently rolled between the fingers can be used to lift out colour delicately and precisely. It is similar in principle to a kneaded eraser, but has a lighter and cleaner touch.

These techniques work with dry pastel types, but the greasy texture of oil pastel is very difficult to erase, and you cannot make erasures to oil or water-soluble pastels that have been treated with a solvent. If you have made errors with these media that cannot be overworked, there is probably no solution but to start again.

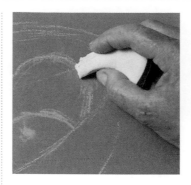

Using a kneaded eraser
Shape the eraser to give a firm edge or point, depending on the quality of the mark you wish to erase and the area it covers. Use gentle dabbing motions to lift the loose colour. A faint trace of the marks may be left on the paper.

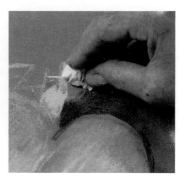

Erasing with bread
Tear off a small piece of bread and shape it into a firm wad. Press it lightly on the pastel surface to pick up loose colour. Once the surplus colour is removed, you can use a fresh piece of bread to rub the surface gently, further erasing the marks.

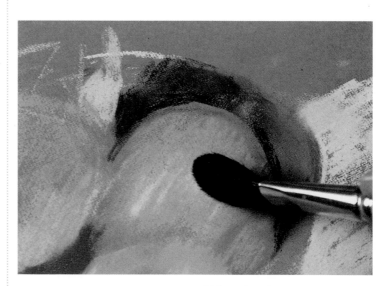

Using a brush
Where you have blocked in colour too heavily, or you wish to open up the surface for overworking, use a brush with soft but firm bristles to flick away the pigment particles.

Frottage

This technique is a means of reproducing the effect of a specific texture by placing your paper over a textured surface and rubbing the pastel stick over the paper. The different features of the underlying texture show up as variations in the pastel colour. According to whether the surface is raised or recessed at any given point, the pressure of the pastel stick varies, and you automatically obtain corresponding changes of tone from dark to light.

Frottage ranges from subtle, evenly patterned impressions taken from a close-textured material such as hessian or fine metal mesh, to the irregular graphic effects thrown up by a coarse wood grain. You can take up a lightly grainy texture from heavy sandpaper, or reproduce the man-made pattern of a sheet of moulded plastic or glass. The character of your rubbing will also depend upon the type of pastel you use.

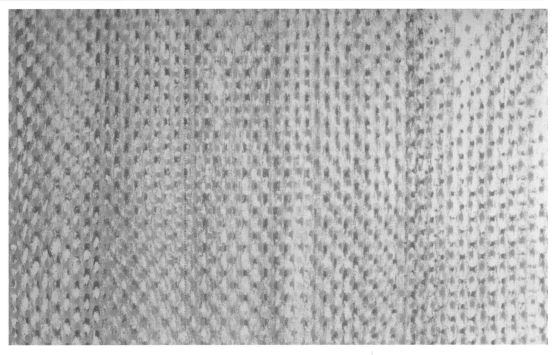

Soft pastels and oil pastels will tend to form a cohesive surface effect, while with hard pastels and pastel pencils it may be difficult to eliminate the marks of the strokes you make on the paper, adding a faint linear bias to the texture picked up from the underlying material. The effects of overlaying pastel colours, using the same or different textures is interesting to experiment with as a way of obtaining areas of broken colour.

Layered colours
Broken colour effects and complex textures can be built up with successive layers of frottaging. This works particularly well with regular textures like a mesh weave or evenly embossed surface. The interwoven effect of this sample is achieved by moving the paper slightly between colours, so each application mixes with the one before.

The effects of frottage are unique to each surface, and sometimes unpredictable. The examples here were achieved by rubbing over (from left to right) architectural stonework, wood grain, rough textured concrete and a slatted wood door.

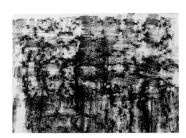
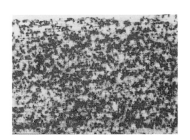
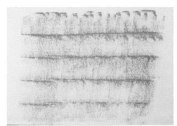

Resist Techniques

Resist methods are based on the incompatibility of oil- and water-based mediums. If you lay down lines or patches of colour using an oil pastel, then brush over it with a thin wash of ink, watercolour or acrylic paint, the greasy texture of the pastel repels the fluid colour – the paint settles into the paper around the oil pastel marks, leaving their colour and texture clearly visible. With repeated applications of both media, allowing the washes to dry in between, you can build up a dense, complex image.

A lightweight pastel stroke leaves parts of the paper grain unfilled, so the paint will settle into irregularities within the pastel colour, as well as round the edges. To get very distinctive, strong-coloured marks, you need to apply the pastel heavily. The best media for this technique if you want to layer the image are inks and liquid watercolours (those sold in bottles).

Some hard pastels have a wax content that makes them of limited use for resist technique. You need to experiment with the range and density of hard pastel marks, as sometimes they do repel the wet colour but also intermittently they absorb it. Soft pastels are ineffective as resist media, as the colour will spread into an overlaid wash (see Wet Brushing, page 58).

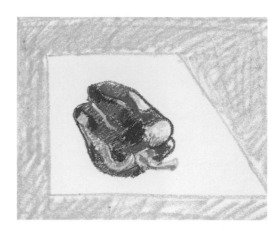

1 Draw an image in oil pastel, using heavy, boldly textured strokes. You can apply as many colours as you wish.

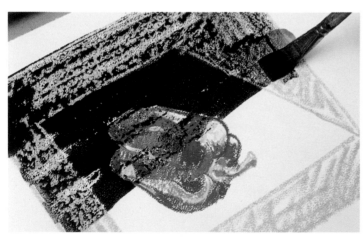

2 Apply a free wash of ink or liquid watercolour, using a large, soft brush to flood the colour easily over the pastel drawing.

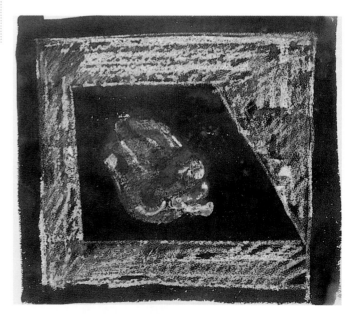

3 As you complete the wash, the liquid colour will settle into the paper grain within and around the pastel marks. You can use a single colour for the overlay, or more than one.

Scratching out

Some particularly dense drawing inks may flood the pastel marks rather than be repelled by them. If this occurs, you can use a knife blade to scratch back the ink when it is dry, retrieving the colour of the underlying image.

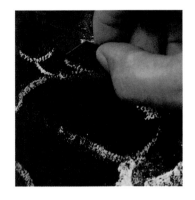

Layering the image

This resist image was built up in several stages with liquid watercolour over oil pastel. The textured pattern of the leaves was first drawn with white, pink and grey pastels, then loose washes of brown and green watercolour were overlaid. When the paint dried, parts of the pastel drawing were reworked and further washes applied, adding blue and red to the colour range. This process was repeated once again to build up the density of colour and texture.

The close-up section below shows how the layering of successive washes creates a more complex background, with free brushwork making an active surround to the leaf forms. Linear detail in the leaf colours was retouched with oil pastel in the final stages.

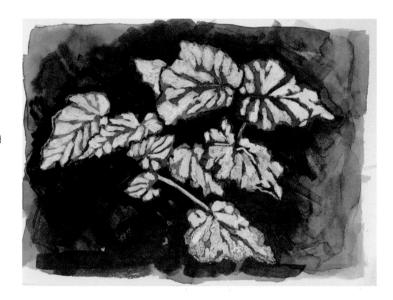

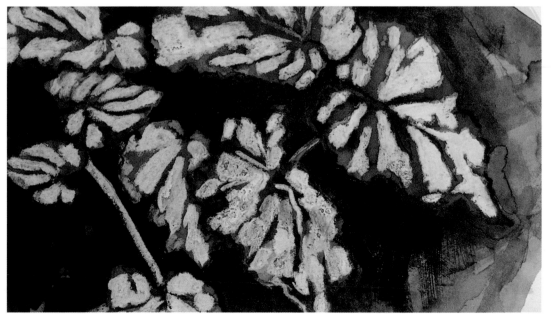

Watercolour and Pastel

The translucency and fluidity of watercolour make an interesting complementary contrast to the opacity and density of soft pastel. Both media have brilliant colour qualities but quite different surface characteristics – in combination they can form images of depth and subtlety that convey particularly well transient effects of light and shade. A mixed-media approach is highly suitable for interior subjects and landscapes that include elements of mood and atmosphere.

The simplest way of combining these media successfully is to begin by blocking in the composition with watercolour washes to establish the main colour areas and the patterns of light and shade. Then, when the watercolour has dried, rework the whole image in pastel to develop detail and emphasize colour accents and tonal contrasts. You can treat this as a layering process, alternating watercolour and pastel work and working the detail more finely at each stage. However, a wet wash will pick up and spread the pastel particles (see Wet Brushing, page 58), so you need to control your reworkings carefully to make sure they enhance the effects rather than muddy the image.

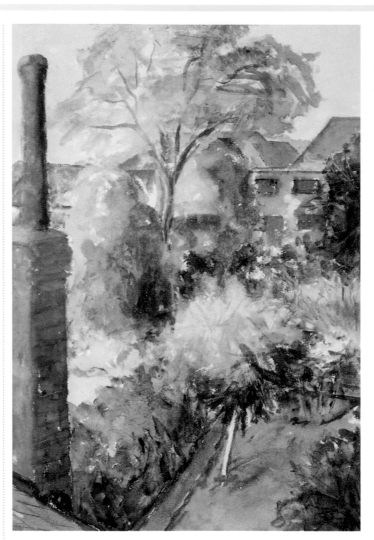

1 In this example, a freely worked but detailed watercolour rendering is laid in as the basis for the composition.

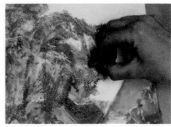

2 Loose, grainy pastel strokes are initially applied over the dried watercolour to develop the complexity of the foliage textures.

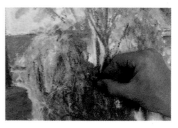

3 The same treatment is applied to all the foliage areas in the painting, gradually building up the colour density with overlaid strokes.

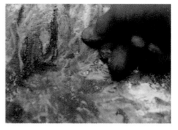

4 In the foreground, where the pastel colour is already thickly worked, the artist introduces some oil pastel work to vary the textures, overlaying it on the soft pastel and partially blending the strokes with finger pressure.

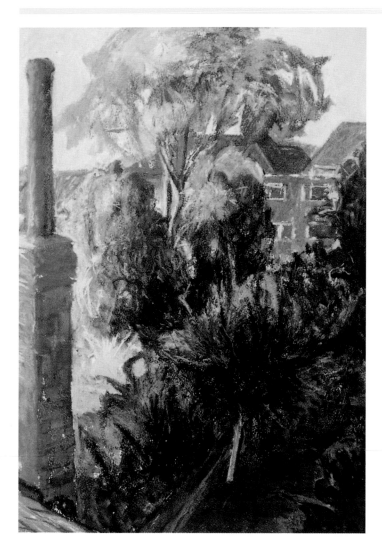

5 In the final stage, patches of shaded pastel are laid into the brickwork in the foreground and buildings in the background to develop colour contrast, textural detail and highlighting.

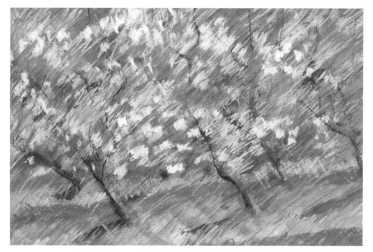

▲ JUDY MARTIN
ORCHARD IN NORMANDY
This watercolour and soft pastel painting takes a different approach, with the pastel strokes used as an overall linear texture to build up a free impression of the blossom trees. To begin with, the pastel was drawn over a watercolour base, but the two media were alternated in successive stages to intensify tones and colours and enhance the effect of light.

Oil Paint and Pastel

Oil pastel can be combined with oil paint to contribute additional linear qualities subtly different from those that can be achieved by brush drawing. Marks drawn directly onto canvas with oil pastel have a grainy quality that can be retained when lightly overlaid with oil paint thinned to a semi-transparent glaze. Alternatively, you can work into a thin layer of oil paint with the pastel tip to develop linear textures and shading – the passage of the pastel stick actually grooves the surface of the paint and also leaves colour traces.

When you are working into wet paint, the medium or diluent used to thin the paint may soften the pastel texture. If you want to achieve harder line qualities, allow the paint layer to begin to dry before adding pastel work.

If you work on paper, or cardboard very lightly primed with acrylic gesso (or even unprimed), the oil paint will dry quickly. Because the paper absorbs some of the oil, it will also have a matt surface, which blends well with the pastel.

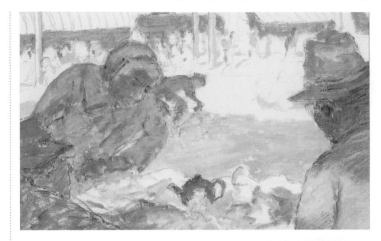

Painting with oil pastel
1 In this example, oil paint is used to block in the basic colour areas, then all the detail is developed with overlaid oil pastel. This picture shows the initial application of paint.

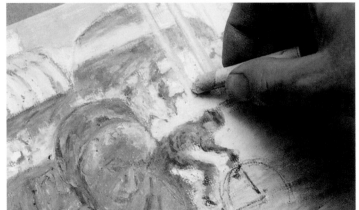

2 Oil pastels are used to work into the colour areas, modelling individual forms and developing the surface patterns and textures in the figures and background. The pastels are manipulated in different ways to create areas of broken colour, as in the woman's hair and scarf, and linear detail such as the awnings and masts of the market stalls.

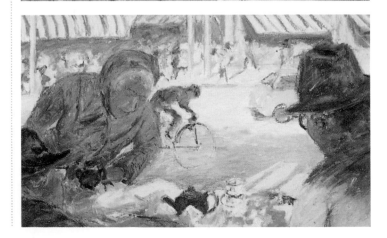

3 The pastel is rubbed into the wet paint and areas reworked to intensify the contrasts of light and shade and draw in the detail in the foreground. Compare this with the first stage, to appreciate how the pastel colours are variously used to emphasize the forms and rhythms of the composition.

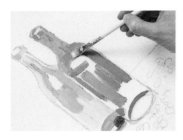

Drawing into oil paint

1 The basic shapes in the still life are drawn with oil pastel on a primed surface. The main colour values are rapidly blocked in with oil paint applied thickly.

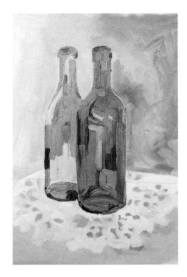

2 The whole image area is covered in the same way, using the paint only at this stage to create a solid rendering of the two bottles and a general impression of the vertical and horizontal planes.

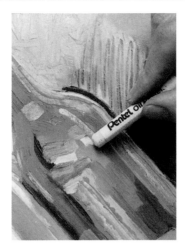

3 Black and grey pastels are used to hatch in the shadow area behind the right-hand bottle. Details of the reflected colours and highlights on the glass are drawn into the wet paint with yellow, green and yellow ochre oil pastels.

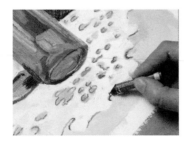

4 In the same way, linear details of the pattern on the lace doily are drawn with black and yellow ochre pastels. The pastel tips are sharpened by shaving them with a knife, to produce a fine line.

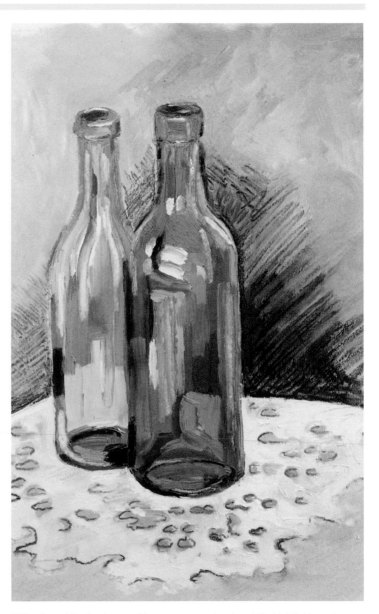

5 Shading of the background is strengthened with black oil pastel, and the rims and bases of the bottles are more strongly defined with pastel lines and accenting strokes. To enhance the tonal contrasts, white highlights and intense black shadows on the bottle glass are brushed in with bold dabs of solid, opaque paint.

Charcoal and Pastel

Charcoal is the medium traditionally used for sketching out the layout of a composition, providing the guidelines for application of colour and tone. In this role it is a useful complement to pastel, particularly soft pastels and oil pastels which you might use to build dense impasto effects over a compositional framework drawn with charcoal. You can create a quite clearly defined charcoal sketch to begin with, then brush away the loose charcoal with a soft paintbrush before introducing the colour work.

Alternatively, you can use charcoal as a more significant visual element to enhance the graphic qualities of a pastel drawing. The textures of charcoal and soft pastel go well together, but charcoal is grittier and can contribute sharp line qualities and hard blacks. To avoid contaminating colours with black dust and charcoal fragments, confine this mixed-media approach to quick sketches and studies, and use frequent, very light sprays of fixative as necessary.

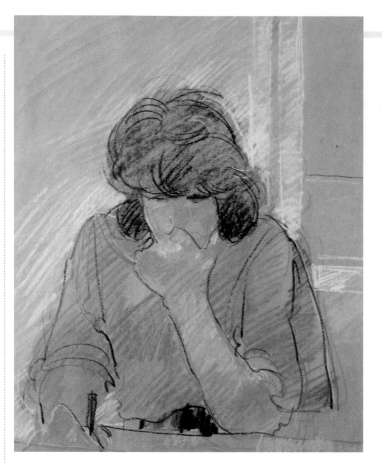

Charcoal over pastel
1 A linear technique is used for this portrait drawing, initially applying charcoal and hard pastel in quick, light strokes to establish the contours of the figure and the broad colour areas.

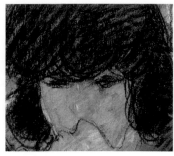

2 The gradual build-up of colour continues, with warm browns and pinks developing the richness of the flesh tones contrasted with cool grey shadows and brilliant white highlights. Charcoal is used extensively to emphasize the dark tone of the hair and to delineate the eyes.

3 In this area of the portrait, the charcoal again signifies linear detail and shadow areas, as in the folds of the pink shirt. It is worked over the pastel colour, which has been applied as loose shading and hatching; then the final highlights and colour accents are touched in with the pastels.

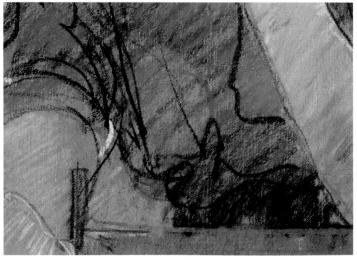

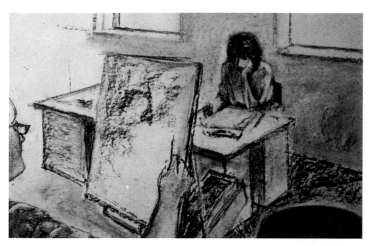

Pastel over charcoal

1 Here the approach is different, with charcoal used to create a detailed monochrome drawing of the subject, which then forms a base for the colour rendering. In the initial drawing, sharp lines are contrasted with loosely worked shading and graded tones. When applying the charcoal, you can work up the dark tones quite heavily. Because it is a very dry medium, it does not clog the paper tooth.

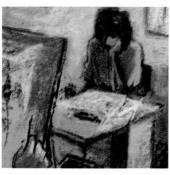

3 The first layers of colour are blocked in quickly using the tip and edge of the pastel stick. At first these show broad colour variations across the whole image. Highlights are applied to counterbalance the dark charcoal tones.

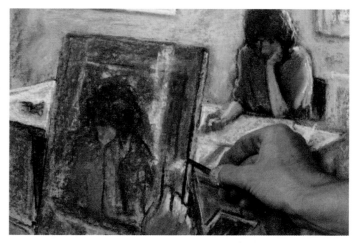

4 As the colours are built up more heavily, charcoal is again used where necessary to redefine the framework of the composition and give emphasis to the forms. It is possible to draw over the pastel and still obtain clean, heavy blacks. In the final stages, the balance of tones is adjusted by applying thick colour with the tip of the pastel stick to develop highlight areas and colour accents.

5 The finished composition has a strong pattern of light and shade. Foreground shapes remain dark, with the pastel used just to tint the blacks, while the light near the windows is conveyed by heavier overlays of colour, the charcoal showing through as a linear framework.

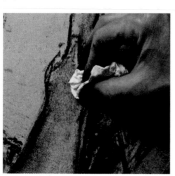

2 Light and mid-tones can be smoothly graded by rubbing the charcoal with a tissue. Dust off the surface and apply a light spray of fixative before starting to apply pastel colour.

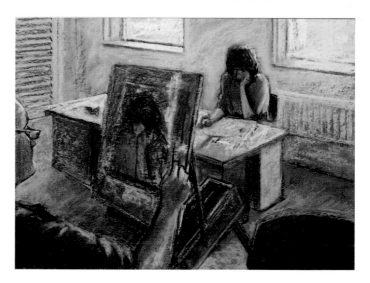

Gouache and Pastel

Gouache and soft pastel are ideal partners for mixed-media work, providing similar colour character and complementary textures. Both are opaque media in which the pure hues and tints are particularly brilliant – gouache lightens slightly as it dries, and its paler colours are highly reflective.

In combining these media, let the gouache do the painting and take advantage of pastel's qualities as a drawing medium to provide additional detail and textural contrast. Exploit linear strokes and massing techniques – for example crosshatching and stippling – that can be integrated with flat washes of gouache, broad brushmarks or heavy impasto.

This is an excellent combination of media for outdoor subjects – landscape and townscape. You can block in the general colour areas with gouache and work over them with pastel to develop the textures and patterns of, for instance, grass, flowers and foliage, or building materials and architectural details. Another good use of pastel in this context is for inserting figures after you have established the main features of your outdoor scene, freely drawn over the dried gouache, and for touching in final highlights and colour accents.

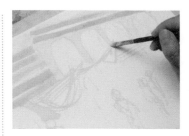

1 The composition is lightly sketched in with a pale yellow soft pastel. Initially, washes of gouache colour are laid into the background area, blocking in the main forms of the building.

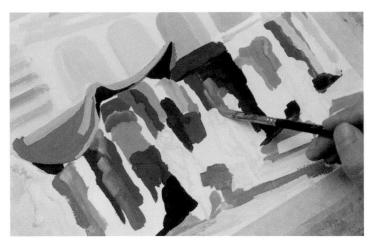

2 Basic shapes and colours in the market stalls and roadway are similarly blocked in. In these early stages the main purpose is to eliminate most of the white paper and create a colourful surface for working over in more detail.

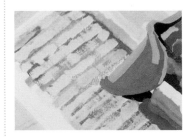

3 The ribbed pattern of the stonework on the left-hand wall is drawn over the dried gouache layer using brown and orange soft pastels. Thicker bands of gouache are overpainted on the same area.

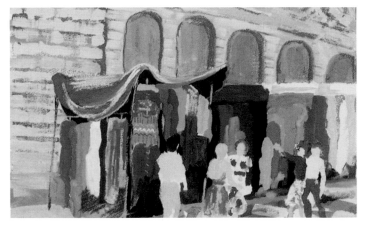

4 The combination of media is freely worked to develop texture and colour overall. With the figures blocked in, all the white paper is now covered, and pastels are used to draw in finer detail on the figures and stalls.

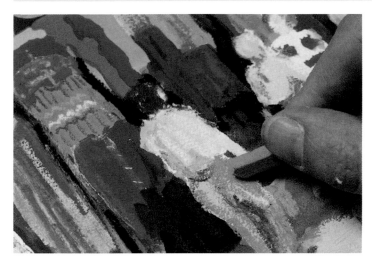

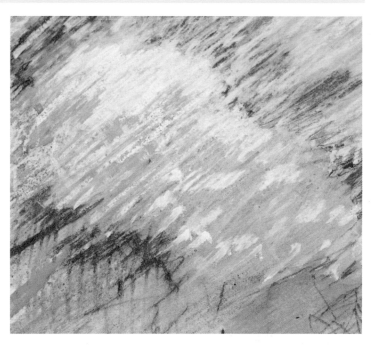

5 Pastel work on and around the figures is quite free and sketchy, but designed to model the forms more solidly and give an impression of greater detail. The grain of the paper is still visible although the pastel is applied over opaque gouache.

6 Pastel is used to enhance the lights and shadows on the roadway. In the background, the proportions of the wall of arches are adjusted using solid gouache applications and broken dry-brushed textures, together with some pastel shading.

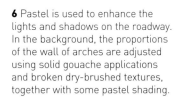

▲ JUDY MARTIN
TREE STUDY
The dense texture of the foliage and complex colour variations have been developed by hatching and scribbling freely into the gouache washes while still damp. This has the effect of binding the pastel particles, giving the marks a heavy impasto character. Pencil was also worked into the surface to create a finer contrast of linear detail.

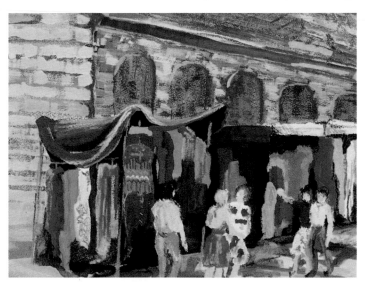

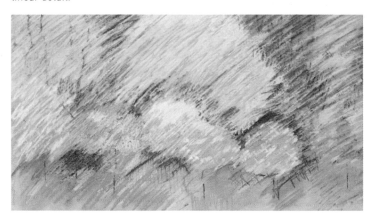

Scratchboard with Oil Pastel

You can use oil pastels to make a kind of scratchboard, or scraperboard. The effect this gives is very different from that of conventional scratchboard, and it is also quite unlike the marks and impressions you make by drawing directly with the pastel stick.

You begin by building up a layer of solid black on the surface of a piece of smooth-finished artboard, using repeated thin applications of waterproof black Indian ink brushed on evenly. Once the ink layer is dry, you scribble hard with a white or light-coloured oil pastel so that the surface is covered with a rich, thick, slightly textured layer of colour. Oil pastel tends to adhere unevenly to the smooth surface, so you are bound to get some minor variations of tone and texture, but aim to cover the ink as solidly as you can.

With the pastel layer complete, you can begin to draw into the surface, using a pointed or hard-edged tool – a scriber, the tip of a large nail or a scalpel blade, for example, or for less sharp effects, the wooden end of a paintbrush. As you scratch into the pastel layer, you reveal the ink, making linear marks that can be true black or greyed, depending on how cleanly you remove the pastel. If you get something wrong, correction is an easy matter – work over the surface again with the pastel and redraw with your scratching tool.

The technique corresponds to ordinary methods of drawing in monochrome, except that you are recovering the black marks from the white surface, rather than laying them on. It is similar to sgraffito (see page 41), but the important factor here is the resilience of the ink surface and the way its density and slight sheen contribute to the final effect of the image.

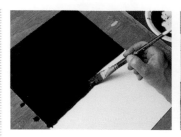

1 Use a firm piece of white artboard with a smooth surface that will not buckle when wetted. Coat the board with black ink, building up the density with two or three applications.

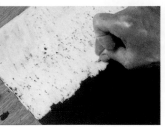

2 Take the paper wrapping off a stick of white oil pastel and rub the pastel firmly over the inked surface, gradually covering the board with a thick layer of white.

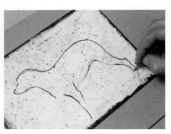

3 Use any suitable tipped or pointed tool – a masonry nail is used here – to draw into the oil pastel, scratching it back to reveal the black underlayer.

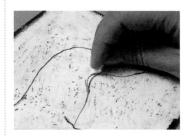

4 If you make an error at any stage, simply reapply the pastel to cover the scratched marks and restore the surface, then rework the drawing.

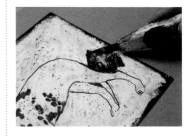

5 To remove larger areas of the pastel coating, scrape it back with the edge of a craft-knife blade. Move it flatly across the surface to avoid digging into the board.

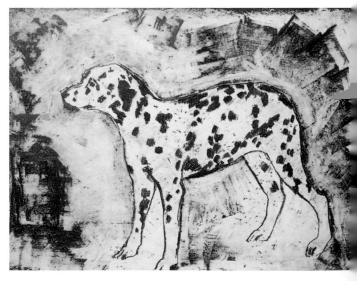

6 As the drawing becomes more detailed, you can adjust the balance of line and tone and develop the textural variation by reapplying pastel and reworking the scratched lines and shapes as required.

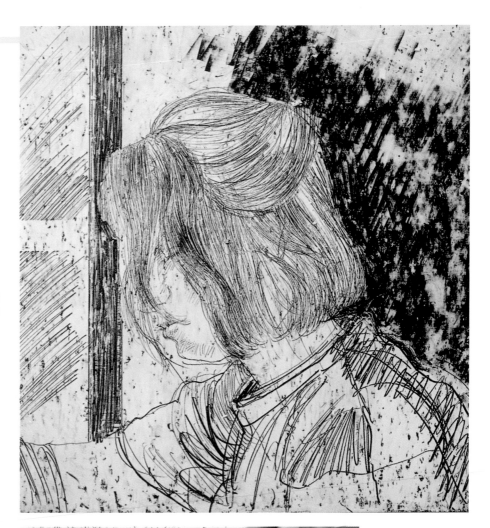

This portrait drawing shows a different approach to working on oil pastel scratchboard, where the main part of the image is drawn only with fine lines, scratched with a carpenter's awl. For contrast, part of the background is scraped back with a knife blade. The technique allows variations of style similar to those you can achieve in pencil drawing.

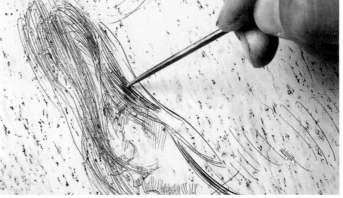

Pencil and Pastel

However dextrous you become in manipulating pastels as drawing tools, it is difficult to sustain a hard, sharp line in this medium. Some subjects suggest a style of rendering in which linear qualities should be combined with a softer technique – seaspray washing over jagged rocks, for instance, or a bird of prey with a sharp beak and glittering eyes mounted on a mass of rumpled feathers. In such cases, pencils can be a useful complement to pastel colours.

Choose relatively soft pencils, those graded from B to 6B. In relation to pastels, of course, even these are fine, hard drawing points, yet they produce a subtle variability of line and appreciably grainy texture that complement pastel qualities. If you are using the pencil only for line work, you can work it into and over pastel colour, and vice versa. If you build up dense pencil shading or hatching, the slightly greasy texture of the graphite will resist an overlay of dry pastel particles.

Use the pencil decisively but delicately. If you allow the point to groove the paper and try to erase any lines, the impressions will show up through pastel worked over the same area. Otherwise you can combine the media very freely. You could explore the combination of line and colour further by trying other point media, such as coloured pencils, felt-tip pens, even pen and ink.

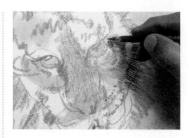

3 Pencil line is also used to sharpen the detail around the eyes and nose, working freely over the pastel colour.

4 As the drawing develops, loose hatching and shading with the pencil builds up the stronger blacks of the tiger's stripes. Variations in the density of the pencil marks create texture and tonal variation.

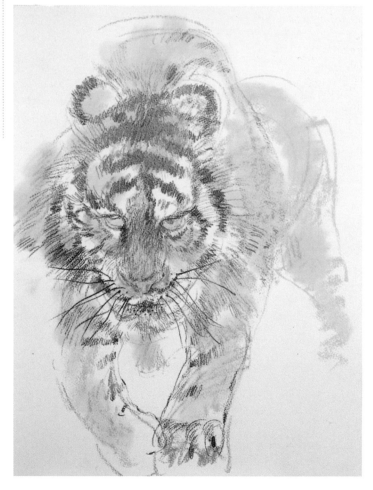

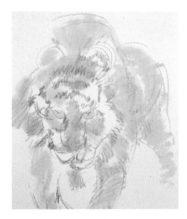

1 The basic form of the animal is blocked in with soft pastel, using linear marks and broad colour areas rubbed with the fingers.

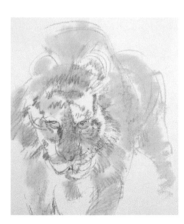

2 A furry texture is built up around the tiger's face with lightweight, feathered strokes of a 2B pencil.

Pouncing

This technique for transferring a drawing from one surface to another is useful if you are going to create a finished rendering based on a sketch or working drawing. It is more suitable for pastel work than the conventional method of tracing down an image, since tracing often involves pressing hard with a pencil or ballpoint pen to transfer the image effectively. This creates a definite outline which may be hard to cover with the pastel, and possibly indents the surface of the paper as well, but with pouncing you use a powder medium to obtain a faint, dotted guideline. This does not affect the quality of the working surface and is easily obliterated as you build up the pastel work.

In the first stage of pouncing, you prick holes at spaced intervals along all the lines in your original drawing. This does, of course, damage the drawing, so if it is one you want to keep, you may prefer to take a tracing of it for this purpose, rather than using the original sheet. For piercing, you can use a stylus or a darning needle – anything that makes distinct but not over-large holes.

You then lay the pricked drawing over the working surface and force a powder medium through the holes to leave faint marks on the surface below. You can use powdered pastel, chalk or graphite – wrap it in a piece of muslin and twist the ends of the muslin to form a little bag, which you dab over the drawing.

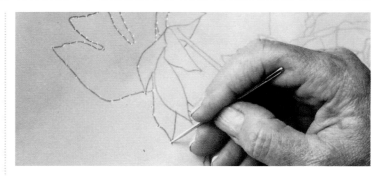

2 Use a large darning needle to prick holes through the tracing paper at regular intervals along the outlines of the drawing.

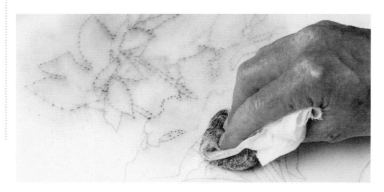

3 Scrape the edge of a soft pastel stick with a knife blade to produce a quantity of powder colour. Wrap the powder in a twist of muslin. Lay the tracing over a clean sheet of paper and dab the bag of powder along the outlines, forcing the colour through the pricked holes.

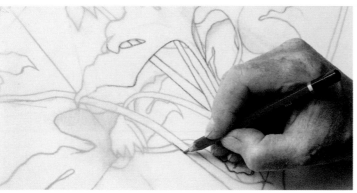

1 Lay a sheet of strong tracing paper over the original drawing and trace off the main outlines of the subject.

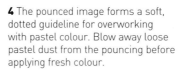

4 The pounced image forms a soft, dotted guideline for overworking with pastel colour. Blow away loose pastel dust from the pouncing before applying fresh colour.

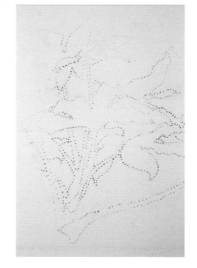

Wet Brushing

The principle of wet brushing is similar to working water-soluble pastels into washes, but in this case you brush clean water over marks made with soft pastels, resulting in a grainy wash or loose mixture of line and wash. If you are working with oil pastels, use white spirit or turpentine. The granular texture of the pastel particles is retained, but their colour tints the water. If you wash over side strokes, for example, you obtain a dense and fairly even washed effect in which the pressure of the pastel on the textured support is still faintly visible. If, on the other hand, you lay down open hatched or scribbled marks and brush over them very lightly, you retain the distinct linear pattern registered through a diffused, pale tint of the original colour. You can also effectively use this technique to create a subtle suggestion of tonal modelling in a line drawing in pastel – for instance, in figure work, to give a gentle shading to the main contours of the face and body.

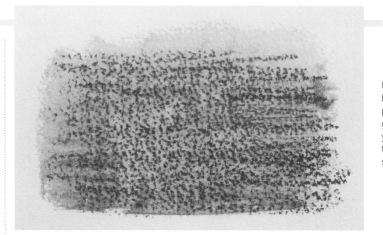

Use a soft sable or synthetic hair brush to flood clean water over soft pastel. Light brushing will leave the grain of the pastel texture visible. If you move the brush outwards from the pastel colour, the tinted water spreads a lighter tone on the paper.

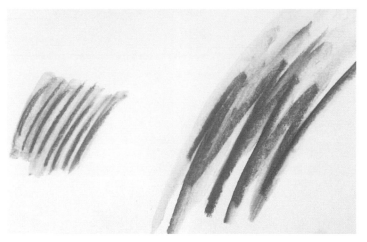

Hatched and scribbled lines stand out clearly against the paler tone of the wet-brushed colour. You can retain the strength of line because the water picks up the colour of the pigment but does not actually dissolve the pastel mark.

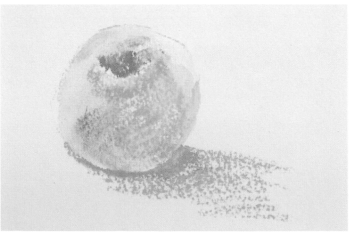

When describing an object, be careful to follow the areas of light and shadow that define the form in the initial pastel drawing, as well as applying local colour. As you wet the colour, brush it outwards from the heaviest tones and let it fade towards the highlight areas.

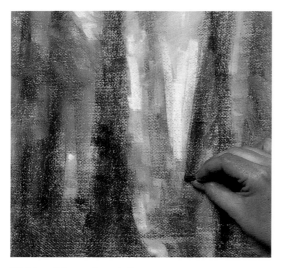

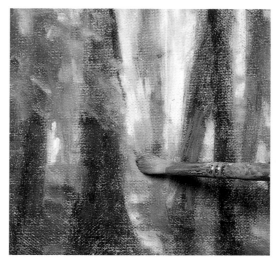

Wet brushing soft pastel
1 Lay down your pastel strokes, in this case broad side strokes.

2 Dip a brush in clean water and begin to spread the colour, taking care to follow the direction of the pastel marks. Clean the brush before applying and wet brushing new pastel colours.

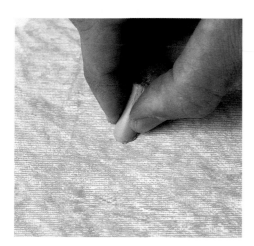

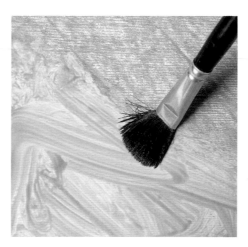

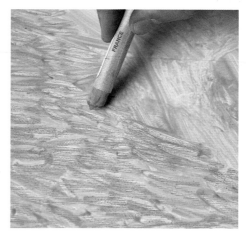

Wet brushing oil pastel
1 Lay down your strokes in oil pastel, in this case an overall shading.

2 Dip a bristle brush in white spirit or turpentine and use this to spread the colour. The pastel can be pushed around like paint – here in a loose, scumbling motion.

3 The spirit makes the pastel greasier, so when you work back into the still-wet paper with dry pastel, the colour will spread easily.

Washes

Water-soluble pastels are formulated to be used either as colour crayons or as the means for achieving soft washes of colour, by dissolving the coloured marks on the support using a brush and clean water. In this way, you can achieve hazy, atmospheric effects of graded, mixed and blended colours, or you can fill a particular area of the rendering quite precisely with translucent, flat colour, The texture and evenness of the wash can vary with the character of the marks you put down to begin with, the amount of water you add, and the way you manipulate the brush. If you want to produce combined line and wash effects, you can work into the wash with the pastels, either while it is wet or after it has dried.

Oil pastels can be treated similarly using turpentine or white spirit as the diluent. An oil spirit medium soaks into paper and can ultimately cause in to deteriorate, so it is advisable to prepare the paper with a coating of size or a light primer, and allow it to dry completely before you work with the oils.

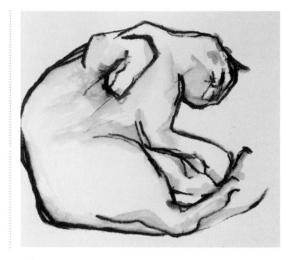

Line and wash
The graphic character of line and wash monochrome drawing, traditionally a pen and ink technique, is imitated here using black water-soluble pastel. The line work has the same fluidity and variation as a pen line, but a chunkier texture due to the thickness of the pastel tip. The grey washes are lightly brushed out from the black line.

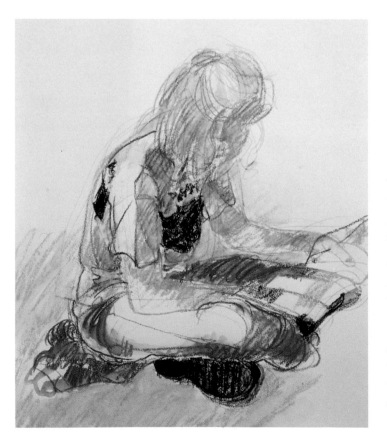

This free figure drawing has been created entirely with water-soluble pastels. When brushed over with clean water, the colour dissolves into an even wash. If you rework linear elements over the damp colour areas, the strokes are more dense and solid due to the moistening of the pastel tip, and less grainy than the dry pastel mark.

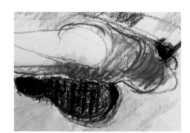

These two details, right, show the range of texture that can be achieved by the wash method. This is a technique that lends itself to a very free way of working and a bold approach to colour.

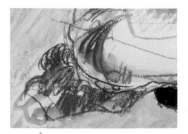

Sfumato

The characteristic of the effect called sfumato (an Italian word meaning "smoke-like") is a soft, hazy quality in which tones and colours merge into each other and build an image without reliance on linear structure or emphasis on edges and contours. Like several commonly used pastel painting techniques, it derives from traditions first established in oil painting, sfumato being particularly associated with Leonardo da Vinci (1452–1519).

Sfumato is not a technique in itself, but a visual quality, and you can achieve the effect by using any of the techniques that enable you to apply controlled, subtle colour transitions – blending, colour gradation, scumbling and shading. If your image has a varied range of tones and a shadowy or atmospheric mood, you can also use careful erasure to lift light out of dark and develop gentle contrasts of light and shade.

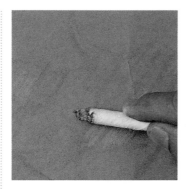

1 The subject is first blocked in with blue and grey soft pastels on a buff coloured paper, using sketchy outlines and loose hatching to define the areas of light and shade. The pastel strokes are softened and spread with a torchon to make the marks less linear and allow the colours to merge.

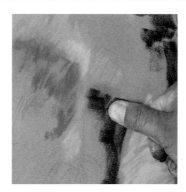

2 The colour areas are gradually built up in lightly shaded layers. Dark tones are smudged with thumb and fingers to create patches of soft shadow.

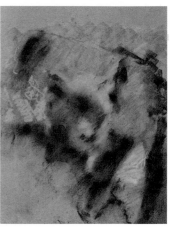

3 The form of the cat's head is developed with dark and light tones. The colours are freely applied using tip and side of the pastel sticks and blended using fingers or torchon as appropriate.

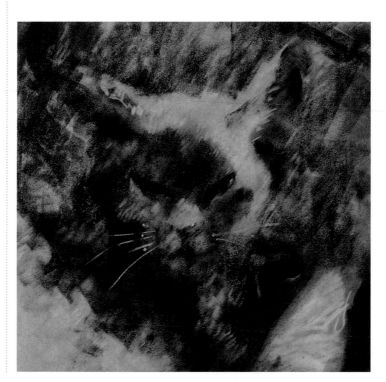

4 In the final stages, the features are drawn with feathery pastel strokes, some blended into the previous colour and others remaining more clearly defined. Although there are no hard edges or distinct outlines, the dramatic use of light and shade makes a highly descriptive impression of form and contour.

Sketching

Sketches serve many purposes and take many forms, from the briefest record of something fleetingly seen to a detailed working drawing that serves as a model for a full-scale composition. Sketching is often particularly associated with outdoor work, and pastels are excellent tools in this case because they combine the attributes of drawing and painting media, easy to handle but providing good colour potential. A box of, say, twelve pastels gives you a versatile colour range in compact, portable form. An alternative method of carrying fragile soft pastels safely for outdoor work is to put them in a jar half-filled with rice grains. This prevents the sticks from snapping and also keeps them clean.

When you are working on very quick sketches, the variety of linear marks (see page 17) that you can make with pastels provides many economical ways of recording shape, form and detail. If you are more interested in broad colour impressions and atmospheric effects, you can combine linear techniques with side strokes and shading.

An important aspect of location sketching is that, however free the drawing, it relates to something real – a landscape or townscape, figure or animal, activity or event. Your techniques will be selected in response to the visual information provided by the subject, and all artists gradually build their own "shorthand" methods of recording these responses.

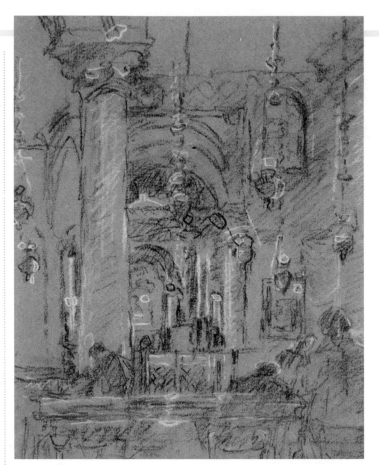

◄ **DIANA ARMFIELD**
INTERIOR OF SAN MARCO, VENICE
(Study for a painting)

Sketching in monochrome is a traditional prelude to working on more complex compositions in full colour. By focusing on essential information such as architectural structure and patterns of light and shade, you can achieve a useful reference sketch quickly. Many artists also take written notes on colour and detail when sketching in conditions that make it difficult to do a colour drawing on the spot.

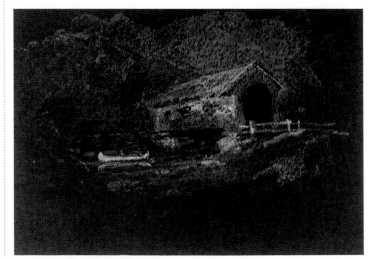

◄ **JOHN ELLIOT**
CANOEING IN VERMONT

The vibrant colour range of pastel is excellent for capturing the mood of a subject with economical techniques. This oil pastel sketch reflects the glowing hues and warm light of early autumn in a countryside resort. Side strokes and patches of shaded colour are combined with linear accents to describe the overall perspective and individual features of the view.

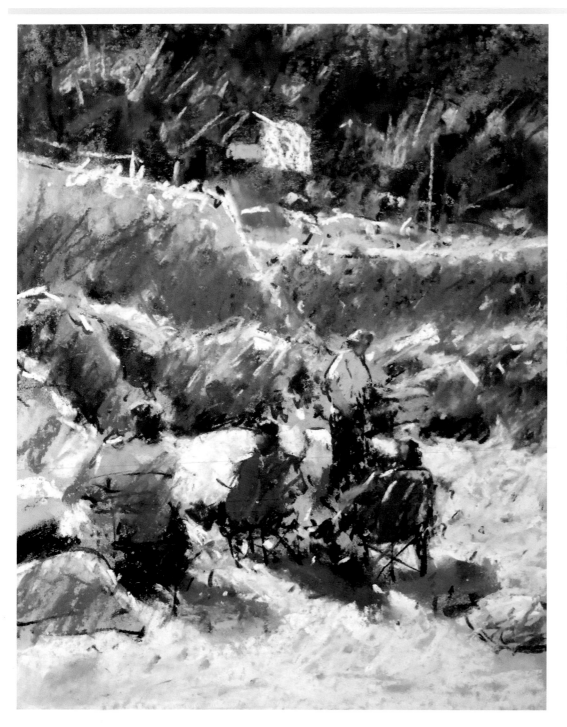

◄ ALAN OLIVER
A DEVON BEACH
By keeping detail to a minimum,
the artist creates a powerful
impression of a beach scene. The
figures are sketched, rather than
drawn, with rapidly applied
strokes. The background is lively,
with lots of overlapping strokes.

Gestural Drawing

The essence of this technique is using rapid and uninhibited movements of the pastel to capture the immediate impression of a subject. It relates particularly well to subjects that have movement – individuals or groups of people, animals, a windswept landscape or pounding sea. It is important to develop a free connection between what you observe and the way you translate it to paper, letting the motion of your hand and arm echo the rhythms of shape, contour and direction. The spontaneity of the approach is lost if you become concerned with individual details.

Gestural drawing is specially successful with soft pastels or oil pastels, because they glide easily across the paper and provide a broad range of surface effects. Exploit your repertoire of linear marks and use loose side strokes to convey massed colour or tone. If you work with hard pastels or pastel pencils, the character of the medium suggests a more sketchy, linear style, using scribbled textures and roughly worked hatching or crosshatching (see page 18) to represent volume and contour.

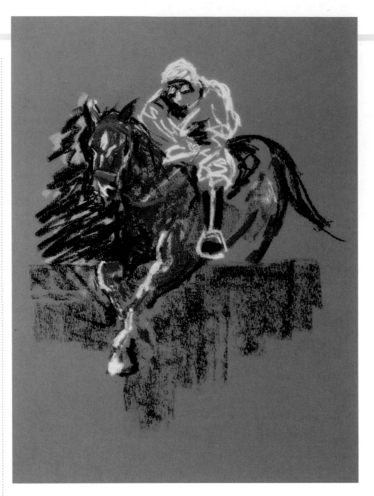

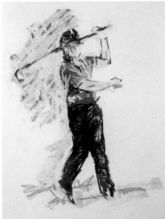

◀ **JUDY MARTIN**
GOLFER

This figure is built up heavily as a network of overlaid marks, with the tip of the pastel used both to shade in colour blocks and describe linear contours that contribute to the sense of movement. The suggestion of a background of blue sky is also worked with scribbled marks rather than laid as an area of flat colour, complementing the dynamic impression of the pose.

◀ **JUDY MARTIN**
OVER THE JUMP

An open, linear style has been used to draw the horse and rider, beginning with free outlines that are gradually reworked to refine the shapes. The colour of the paper gives a coherent background to the rapidly laid marks. Broader sweeps of colour are added with side strokes and loose hatching to give the image a sense of depth and solid form.

▼ **JUDY MARTIN**
MOVEMENT STUDIES

Sequential movement can be studied in simple outline drawings, letting your hand follow freely the rhythms of the form. Each of these sketches was done in a matter of seconds, as a means of studying the motion rather than aiming for a definite image.

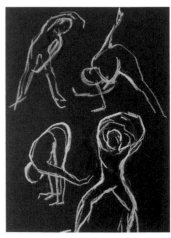

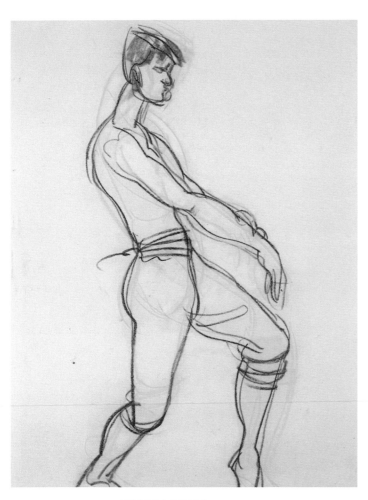

▲ GEORGE CAYFORD
T'AI CHI EXERCISE
Fluid contour lines capture the
essence of the pose and also
describe the roundness of the
limbs and body, where the artist's
hand lets the pastel tip flow easily
around the forms. The movement
sequence is described here using
successive colours as elements of
the pose slowly change.

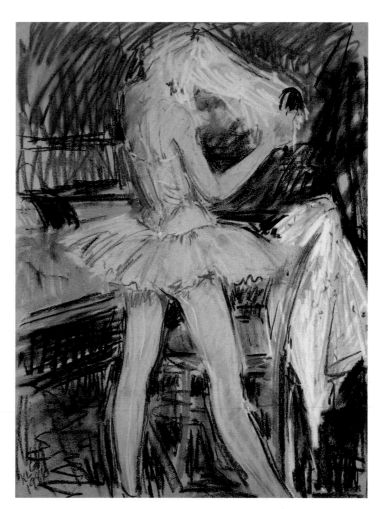

▲ KAY GALLWEY
BALLET DANCER
Active treatment of every area of this image
enhances the impression of space and form.
Directional marks are used to indicate the
structure and detail of the background location,
to describe the textures of the dancer's dress
and hair and to suggest her movements. Visual
contrasts are created between some strokes that
are fragile or harshly linear and others that are
broad and richly grained.

Masking

A mask is simply something that protects the surface of the paper in an area that you are not working on, but masks can be used in a positive way to give a clean edge to coloured shapes or to a whole image. There are several types of masking material, but because of the fragility of pastel work, materials designed to adhere to the surface, such as masking film, tape or masking fluid, are not suitable.

Simple paper masks can be used to outline shapes that you are completely filling with colour by techniques such as shading, side strokes or dry wash. Just cut the shape out of tracing paper, layout paper or thin cartridge and hold it down on the working surface while you apply the colour. Similarly, you can make a paper frame for the whole image area if you want to keep the borders clean. To create a hard edge when colouring, for instance, the corner of a building, simply hold the edge of a paper sheet down the line representing the junction of two planes and work up to it with the pastel strokes.

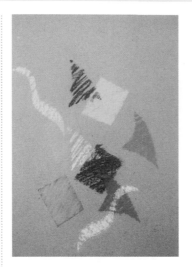

This abstract pattern shows the range of different textural effects you can obtain by working into and around masked shapes, varying the density of the pastel strokes and overlapping colours.

Simple shapes cut out of pieces of paper form stencil-type masks that can be "filled in" with different qualities of pastel colour, creating relatively hard-edged shapes.

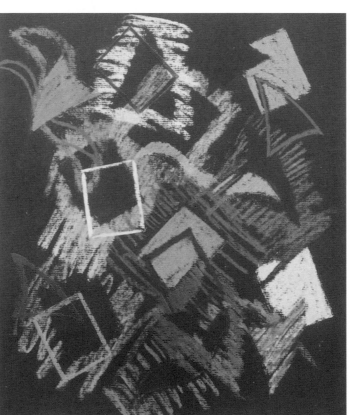

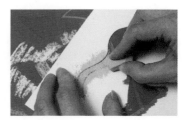

1 When applying colour within a masked shape, keep the direction of the pastel strokes consistent and work over the edges of the mask to ensure that the whole area is coloured.

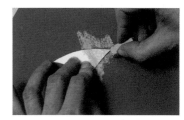

2 The cutout from inside the stencil can be used as a mask to form a negative of the original shape.

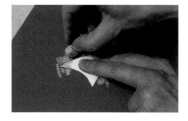

3 To keep the shading around the masked shape consistent, hold the mask down firmly while angling your fingers to gain access to the complete outline.

Fixing

The question of whether or not to use fixatives, and when, causes some controversy among pastellists. The brilliance and fragility of the pigment particles clinging to the working surface are regarded by some artists as essential characteristics of pastel work. Fixatives may be considered to degrade both the colour and texture of soft pastels. However, careful fixing need not spoil the surface qualities, and you may feel that any disadvantages are offset by the protection that fixative gives to your work, both during its stages of development and when it is finished.

The key to successful fixing is to use the fixative sparingly. Overwetting the surface can cause the pigment particles to merge, muddying the texture; it can encourage strong colours to "bleed" through overlying tints; and it does tend to darken colours slightly. But if you apply a light layer of fixative at successive stages of the drawing, it enables you to overwork colours freely and keep the hues, tones and individual marks distinct and clean. Fixing again when the work is finished prevents accidental smudging, powdering or flaking.

If you are working on a light or medium-weight support, you can spray the fixative on the back of the paper. It will penetrate enough to gently dampen the pastel and make it more secure. If you definitely prefer to do without fixative, try "fixing" the surface of a finished work by laying a sheet of tissue over it and applying even pressure to push the pastel particles a little more firmly into the paper grain.

Aerosol cans of fixative are convenient and are usually now environment-friendly. Some artists still prefer using a mouth diffuser spray to apply fixative from a bottle, but you do get a more reliably even spray from an aerosol.

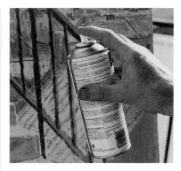

Spraying fixative
Make a quick test spray first to check the nozzle is clear and the spray quality even. Hold the can about 30cm (12in.) from the paper and spray from side to side, covering the whole area. Avoid overspraying, as this wets the surface and may cause colours to run or mix.

Fixing in stages
Some artists like to use a light fixative spray at intervals throughout the work, even in the early stages, to seal the surface before application of further colour layers.

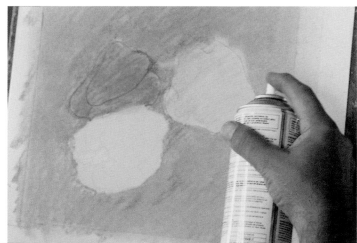

Spraying from the back
Use this method only on light and medium-weight papers. Apply the spray evenly and sparingly as described above, covering the whole of the back of the paper.

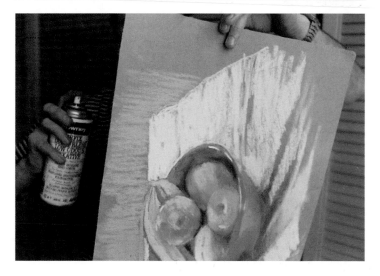

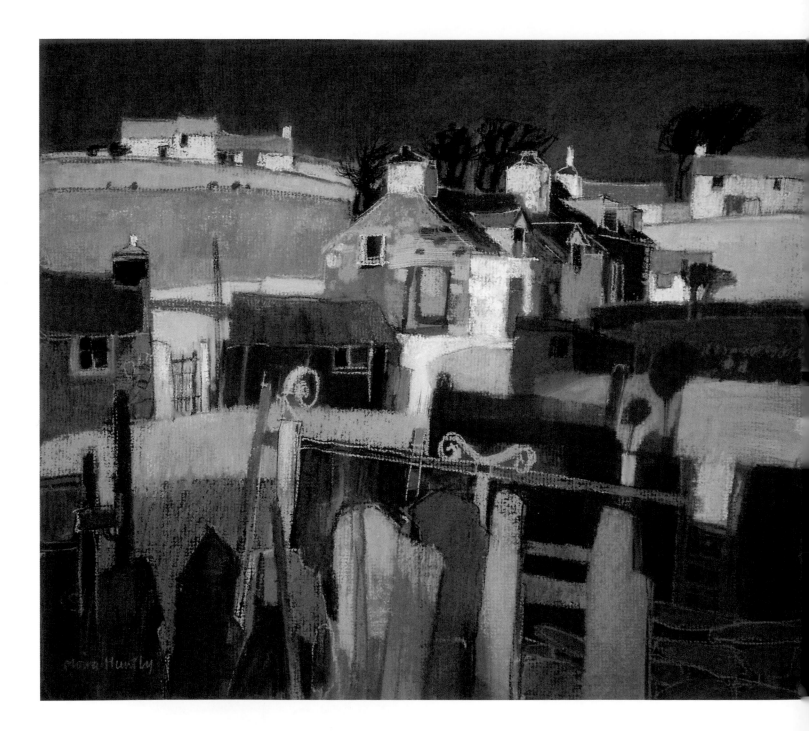

Themes

Any object, person, event or situation is material for the artist, so neither the themes chosen for this section nor the interpretations illustrated are intended to be definitive of their categories. The images have been selected to show the potential of pastel work as well as the ways in which the artists have employed the technical range of the medium to match different elements of a subject and develop a personal style. All artists, whether beginners or established professionals, can learn something by looking at the work of others. The basic themes in art are by now standard and it is difficult to arrive at something new in a general sense. The continuing variety of work in all genres comes from the fusion of observation and technique that is unique to every individual.

This gallery of images is a learning tool that can be used in the same way as the techniques section, to pick out the elements of pastel rendering that you find specially effective and to find out something about how they were achieved. Detailed analysis of the pictures enables you to cross-refer easily between the themes and the techniques, providing a comprehensive guide to the versatility of pastel as a combined painting and drawing medium.

◀ MOIRA HUNTLEY
PEMBROKESHIRE FARMYARD
The higgledy-piggledy arrangement of the buildings belies the underlying order of the composition. Everything is carefully placed and balanced – not only the shapes of the buildings, but also the blocks of colour and the way that they inter-relate and help the viewer's eye to travel around the picture.

Landscape

Landscape seems to be virtually the ideal subject for pastel work. The range of linear marks and massed textures that you can obtain corresponds to the variety of shape and form in nature, while the brilliant colours of pastels and the subtle ways of mixing them are excellent for interpreting natural effects of light and atmosphere. The tradition of working on coloured grounds is also very helpful in landscape drawing and painting, giving an overall tone to the image that can represent the broad spread of earth or sky, or the base colour of grasses, foliage or stretches of water.

Subject matter

The landscape theme encompasses a wide range of individual subjects and landscape features – orderly vistas of patchworked agricultural land, the rough spread of open heathland or marshes, the dense broken colour effects of wooded hillsides or rocky cliffs, a bleak, stony seashore or glistening sandy beach. Each of these landscape views also contains a wealth of individual details that might form your main focus within the general theme – for instance a single unusual tree could draw your attention to a particular area of landscape.

Broadly, landscape can be defined as a natural rather than man-made environment, but this does not exclude constructed features such as farm buildings or country houses, roadways and bridges, walls and fences. Furthermore, for the town-dweller, the local landscape may be sculptured parkland, formally planted gardens, or just the small pockets of green space always to be found in urban sites.

Working methods

The specific aspects of landscape that you choose relate to availability and your preferred working methods. Some people are inspired by the fact that they live in beautiful countryside; others have to travel to particular locations if they want to work outdoors, meaning that the extent of the work is restricted by time and weather conditions. The traditional approach to landscape painting is to make outdoor sketches and then return to the studio to work up finished paintings – this is a good approach with pastel as you can use the same medium for your sketches as for the more elaborate work, giving yourself the right kind of cues on colour and texture.

Many contemporary artists will mix sketch references with photographic material. You have the widest options if you take the photographs yourself, as this allows you to select viewpoints and record various details, but you may also find postcards and magazine features useful to remind you of specific locations or the general character of a certain type of landscape.

▶ PATRICK CULLEN
TUSCAN LANDSCAPE

To create the variety of the dense foliage in the foreground, the artist freely combines areas of broken colour with a variety of linear marks, building a complex, rich impression of colour and texture. The indication of space and distance in the receding landscape is achieved both by simplifying the shapes and textures and by massing subtly cool green, mauve and blue tints in the far-off fields and hills that contrast with the warmer, more vibrant hues of the trees in the foreground. These are linked by the sharper greens and yellows that travel right through the image, enhancing the composition's rhythmic interplay of curving shapes.

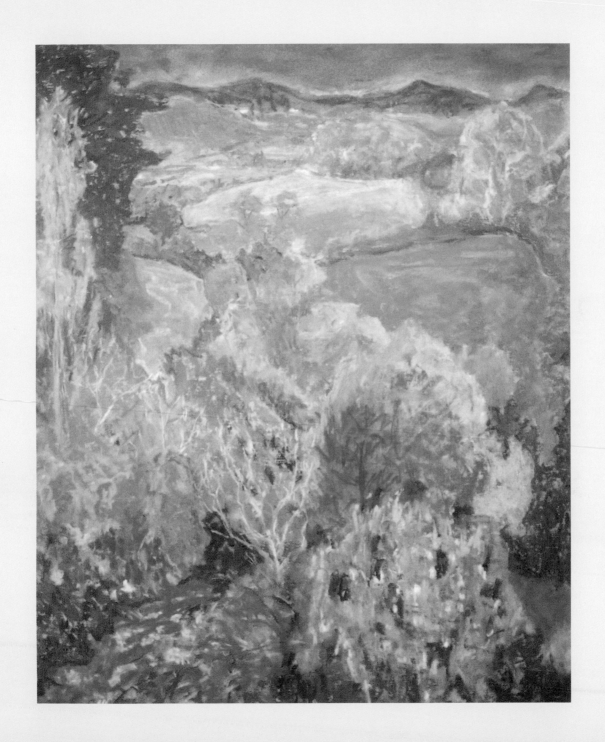

Space and Distance

When you are attempting to contain the huge vista of a landscape on a small piece of paper, one of the most important elements is the position of the horizon line. A low horizon gives you less actual space within which to arrange the details of the landscape, but it creates an effect of great distance. A high horizon may give more prominence to the foreground setting, with the sense of recession more compressed toward the horizon itself; or it may indicate that the land is actually rising, so that much of the view is above your eye level.

Elements that form a linear framework within the image create space by indicating a direction – for example lines of trees or the patterns of ploughed and planted fields converging toward the horizon. With pastel you can use the line qualities of the medium to emphasize these visual cues. The scale and emphasis of the marks you make also contribute to defining space and distance – distinct, bold strokes and large shapes will tend to come forward, forms with indistinct contours seem farther away.

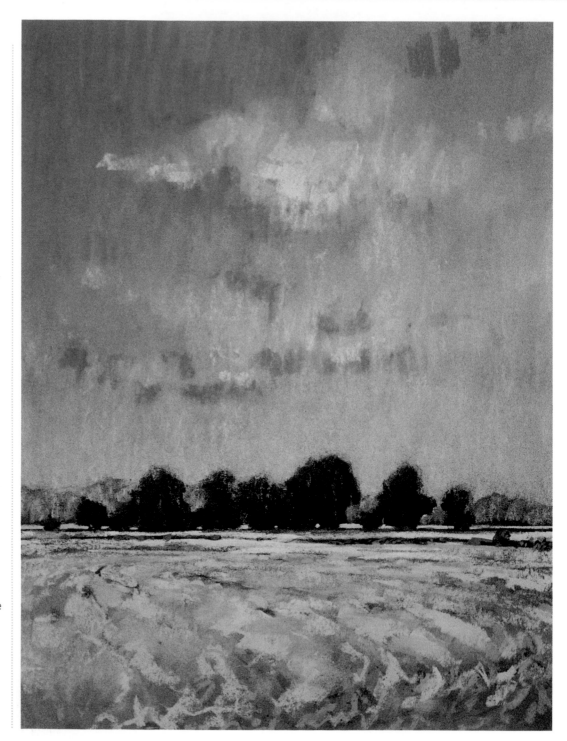

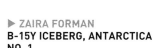 GEOFF MARSTERS
REACH FEN
Sky and land are described with broken colour, the directions of the pastel strokes emphasizing the spatial division. The sense of distance is enhanced by the shadowy tree line at the low horizon, throwing forward the solid, dark tree shapes.

▶ ZAIRA FORMAN
B-15Y ICEBERG, ANTARCTICA NO. 1
In this large-scale work (the drawing is 183cm/72in. square), the iceberg occupies a relatively small area but the composition is perfectly balanced, with the solidity of the iceberg, positioned "on the third", contrasting with the huge expanse of sky and the sliver of sea at the base. The light playing on the ice brings the image to life and offsets the dark and sombre mood of the sky and sea.

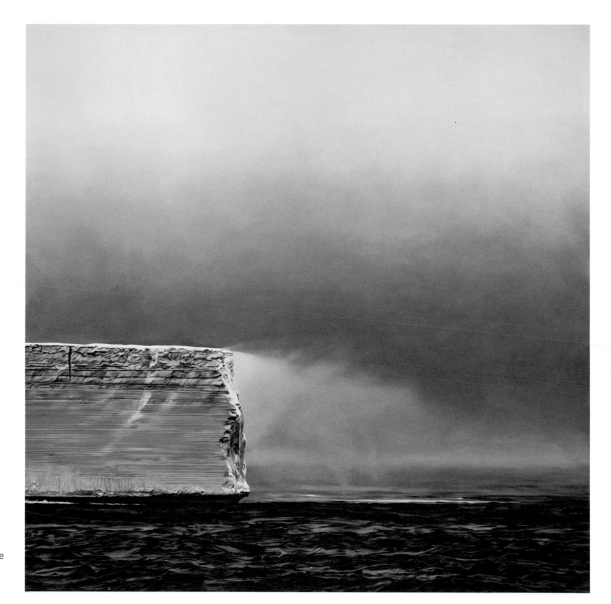

▶ CHRIS NEALE
ENLLI

With the solid, single-storey cottages depicted as simple shapes and the clouds drawn as loose, swirling scribbles of white, this painting has a naïve, almost childlike, quality. Nonetheless, the use of broken colour skilfully captures the ruggedness of the landscape. Although the whitewashed cottages are the main subject, the pathway leading down to the sea draws our eye through the painting to the island in the distance, enhancing the feeling of isolation.

▼ ROSALIND CUTHBERT
BLUE HILLS

The abstract shapes presented by a high mountain range are interpreted as rich masses of colour and texture, using a combination of watercolour and pastel laid over an acrylic and whiting ground. Additional contouring and linear texture are developed with charcoal.

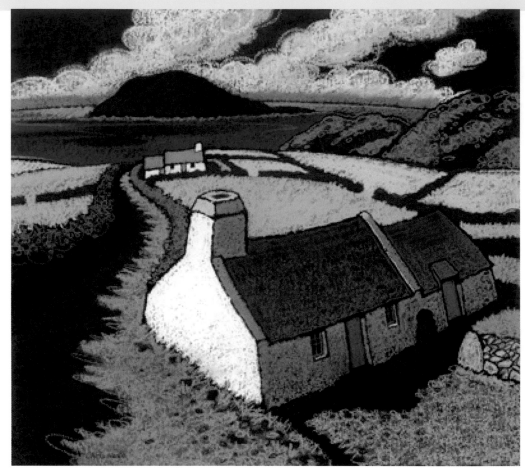

▶ DAVID PRENTICE
COLOURED COUNTIES – LAURA'S WAR

A high viewpoint creates an unusual configuration of land and sky, freely laid in with bold side strokes and linear marks. The strong impression of light and atmosphere is enhanced by the interplay of warm and cool colours, pure hues and neutral tones, and the technique of gestural drawing gives the whole picture surface an active, rhythmic unity in which the divisions between land and sky are sometimes emphatic, sometimes ambiguous.

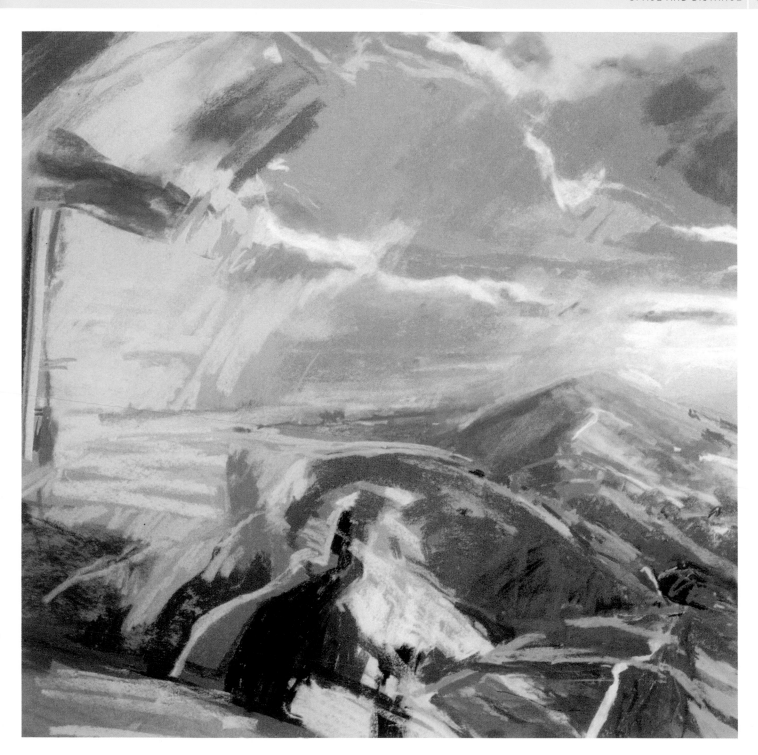

Seasons

Each season of the year has its own characteristics, but since you cannot compare them at the same time, a clear sense of seasonal atmosphere comes from careful observation of actual qualities of light, colour and landscape structure.

Autumn is a favoured time for colour studies; the colours of the trees can be sensational in themselves, and are often enhanced by a rich, warm light. Winter is a less inviting time to work outdoors, either drawing or observing the landscape, but it has its particular visual excitement in the skeletal forms of plants and the strange colour range of lights and shadows on snow. The versatility of pastels makes them equally appropriate for emphasizing the calligraphic qualities of winter landscape or expressing the dense massing of colour, light and shade.

Seasonal character can also incorporate a mood, often relating to weather conditions: landscape rarely appears bleak under brilliant summer sunshine, but heavy storm clouds can make gentle pastoral land seem suddenly threatening.

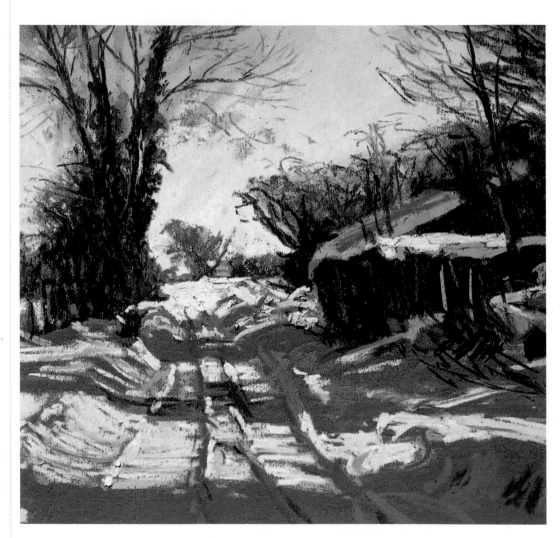

▲ MARGARET GLASS
SUN AND SHADOWS
The abrasive tooth of glasspaper allows the soft pastel to be applied in heavy impasto strokes. In the foreground, the strokes are loosely worked, the warm brown ground contributing significantly to the colour range of the lights and shadows on the snow. The brilliant light effect is created with an interplay of warm and cool colours – there is no pure white amongst the pale tints in the snow.

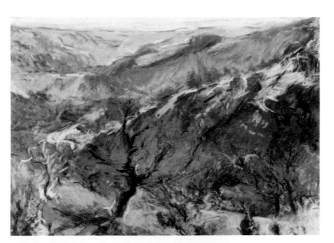

◀ SALLY STRIDE
OAK IN WINTER
This is a colourful interpretation of
winter landscape, but the seasonal
atmosphere is cleverly conveyed
by using a palette entirely
composed of cool and cold colours.
Pale blues and mauves are
typically cold, but here even the
reds and yellows are selected to
inject crisp, clear tints rather than
dense, saturated colours. The
warmest note is reserved for the
strong red-brown woven into the
linear structures of the foreground
trees, which create the focal point
of the composition.

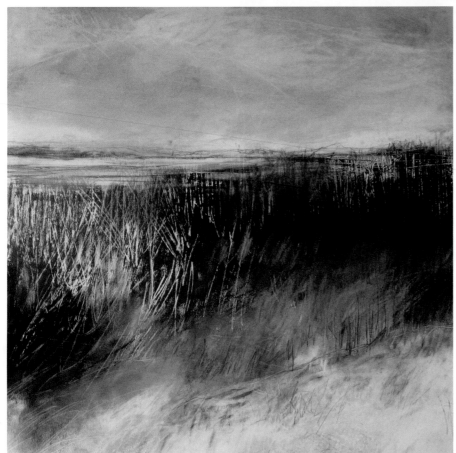

◀ JANINE BALDWIN
STARK HEDGEROWS IN WINTER
Charcoal, graphite and pastel are
all used in this image. The artist
began by using a blunt pencil to
make grooves in the paper, and
then applied a layer of pastel; the
grooves remain white, which adds
another layer to the work and
creates the texture of the bare
hedges. An eraser was also used
to clear spaces on the paper and
leave behind soft traces of colour.

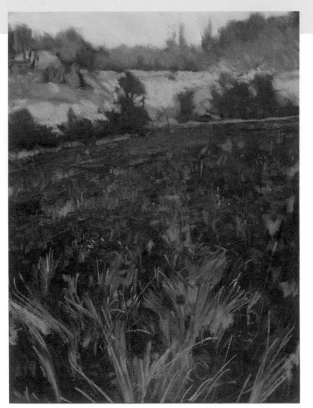

◄ **DAVID NAPP**
POPPIES IN PROVENCE
Densely massed, warm colouring beautifully reproduces the carpeting effect of the poppy field, played off against cooler acidic hues in the background landscape. The marks are differently weighted to bring out detail in the foreground.

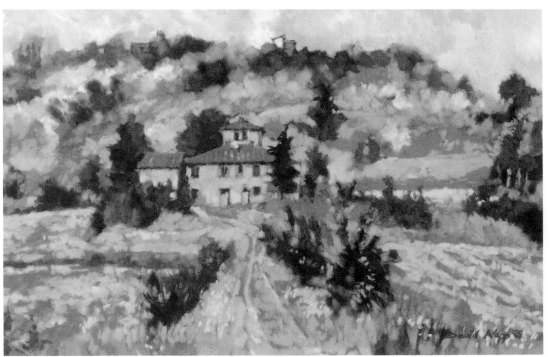

◄ **DAVID NAPP**
FARM TRACK IN TUSCANY
The technique in this soft pastel painting is very consistent, using short, broad strokes to mix and overlay small patches of colour that gradually coalesce into distinctive shapes and forms. The selection of colours evokes gentle warmth in the landscape, but the sky remains cool, again suggesting a spring-like mood.

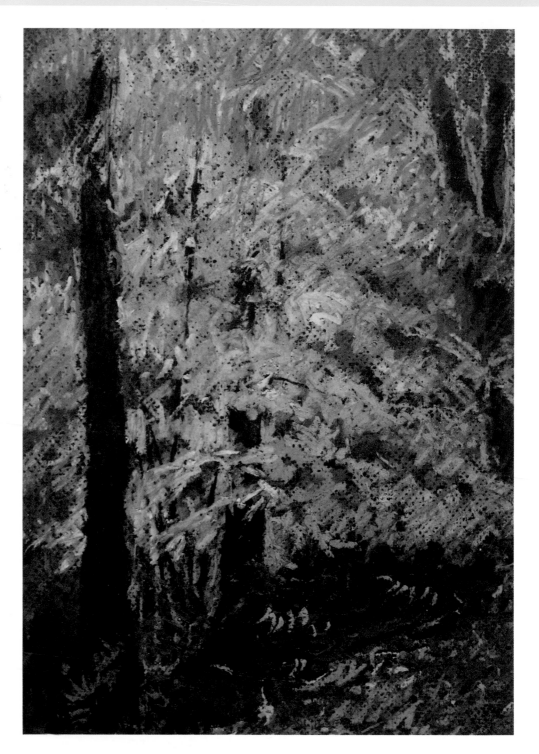

▶ JOHN ELLIOT
AUTUMN NEAR THE ARTIST'S STUDIO
In pastel work it is often advisable to give full rein to the intensity of colour, especially when the technique is free and bold. Oil pastel is used here to develop an active network of linear marks, where strong contrasts of colour and tonal values allow the form and texture of the foliage to emerge. A dark, heavily textured ground contributes to the broken colour effects, although in places the pronounced grain of the paper is concealed by thick impasto dashes and streaks of colour.

Trees

Trees can either be viewed as part of the general population of a landscape or as special features for close study. They have a fascinating amount of variation in their natural shapes, textures and colours, according to the characteristics of the individual species and the seasonal changes they undergo.

While botanical identification is not an essential feature of tree studies, it is important to pay attention to specific visual qualities such as typical outline, branch structure, leaf shape and colour. The more you analyse the particular qualities, the more you can develop the richness and detail of a tree "portrait" or give definition and contrast to a study of massed trees.

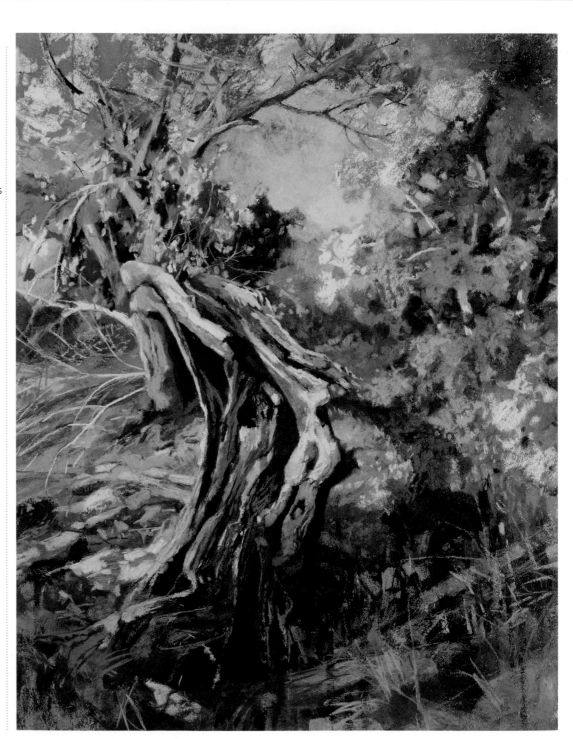

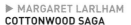 **MARGARET LARLHAM**
COTTONWOOD SAGA
The broad trunks, deeply fissured bark and brilliant autumn foliage are distinctive features of mature cottonwood trees and the artist has captured the character of the trees beautifully. The use of complementary colours – the orangey-yellow of the foliage against the bright blue of the sky – adds to the impact.

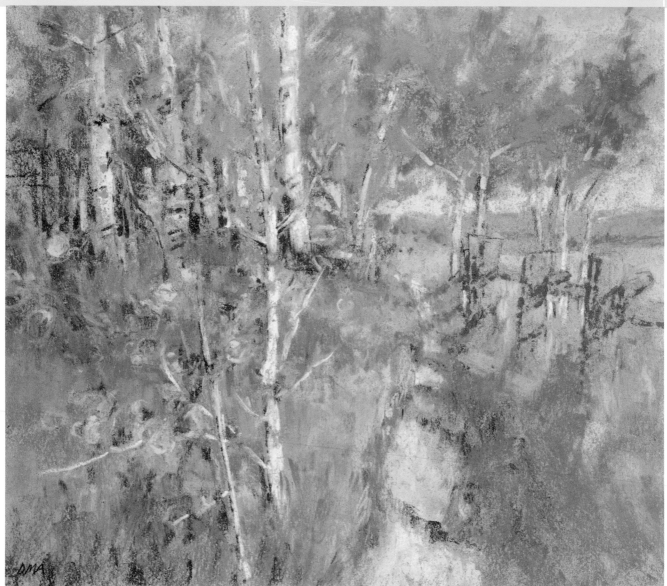

▲ DIANA ARMFIELD
ASPENS ALONG THE PATH IN THE ROCKIES
This image conveys very precisely the detail and character of the slender aspens, and demonstrates how the build-up of many small pastel strokes constructs the impression of form. The soft pastel is handled loosely and economically, blocking in areas of grainy colour and developing textural detail with a variety of linear marks. The cool hues dominant in the painting are offset with discreet accenting in clear pink.

▶ **JUDE TOLAR**
MORNING ASPENS
Broken colours are a really effective way of capturing the effect of the sunlight streaming through the trees. Although there is no obvious focal point, the negative spaces – the gaps between the trees – are as important to the composition as the trees themselves, as they allow our eye to meander around the scene.

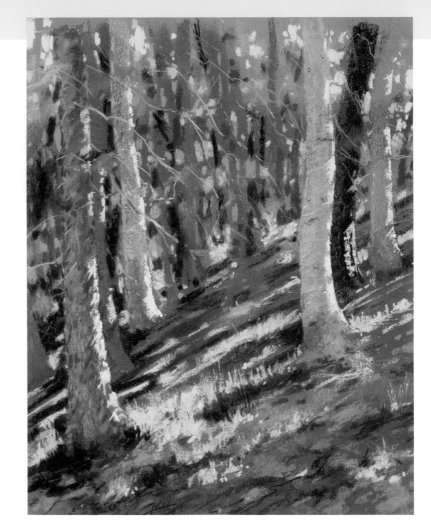

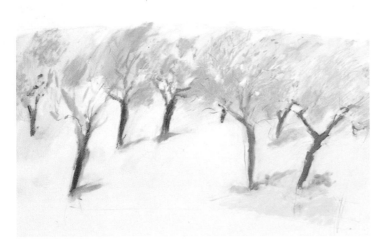

◀ **JANE STROTHER**
OLIVE TREES, MONTECCIO
A cultivated tree planting creates an interesting alignment of forms. This free oil pastel sketch focuses the interaction of the angled trunks and foliage masses, eliminating incidental detail. The pastel is rubbed and blended to create basic colour areas, overlaid with linear marks and loose hatching and shading.

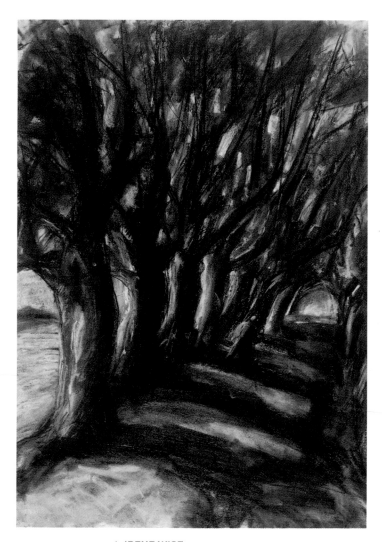

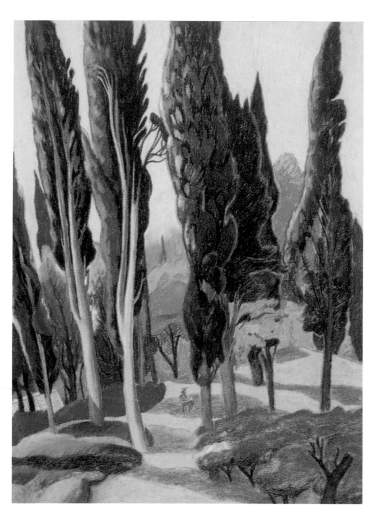

 IRENE WISE
TWICKENHAM RIVERSIDE
The linear quality of hard pastel is
exploited in structuring the dense
network of tree branches and
developing their shadowy tones.
Where colour areas are more broadly
blocked in, the medium has a harsher
grain than that of soft pastel. This
suits the threatening mood of the
composition, described with strong
blacks and a limited colour palette.

▲ ROSALIND CUTHBERT
CYPRESSES
The naturally elegant, elongated forms
of these trees are stylized into distinctive,
solid shapes, using dense shading in soft
pastel to introduce the colour variations.
The vertically of the columnar forms
is thus emphasized, and the inclusion
of the tiny figure at the centre of the
composition creates a point of scale
that also enhances their grandeur.

Foliage, Flowers, Fruit

The immense amount of detail contained within any landscape view can be focused more closely in individual studies of foliage, flowers and fruit. This is an opportunity to experiment technically, and find out how the different kinds of pastel marks convey the extraordinary range of natural leaf and flower forms.

Because the shapes, textures and colour nuances in landscape are so complex, it is often tempting to settle for a broadly impressionistic style that creates a striking image but glosses over the characteristic detail of individual elements. In choosing a particular feature of landscape for more intense study, you can deal with the smaller subtleties of form and colour, acquiring information that will feed back into your broader landscape views.

Even when you limit yourself to an individual subject of this kind, there are still many different aspects to it, and your representation need not be comprehensive or "realistic". Look for the essential details and qualities that enable you to produce a convincing account of your own visual impression.

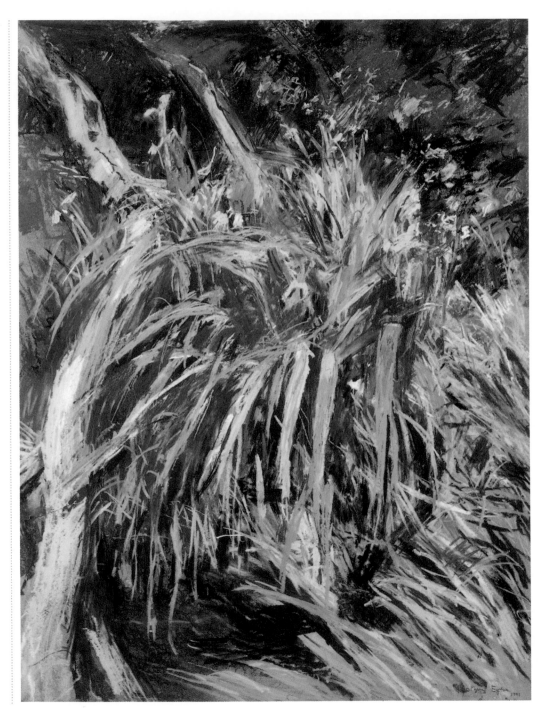

◀ ANTHONY EYTON
IRISES
The mass of foliage is freely translated with gestural drawing, but confident handling of the complex structure and varied colour range produces a striking description.

▶ GEOFF MARSTERS
CHERRY TREE IN BLOSSOM
A consistent pattern of small, hooked linear marks describes variations of texture and local colour, relying on the balance of colour to define form.

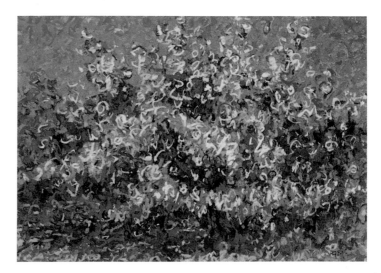

▼ JILL STEFANI WAGNER
ARANCIA
Soft pastels are a wonderful medium for capturing the delicate surface of fruits such as these, as you can create very subtle blends of colour. This drawing was done on terracotta-coloured pastel paper; very little of it can be seen in the finished work, but it helps create the overall colour mood and contributes to the interplay of light and shade, colour and form.

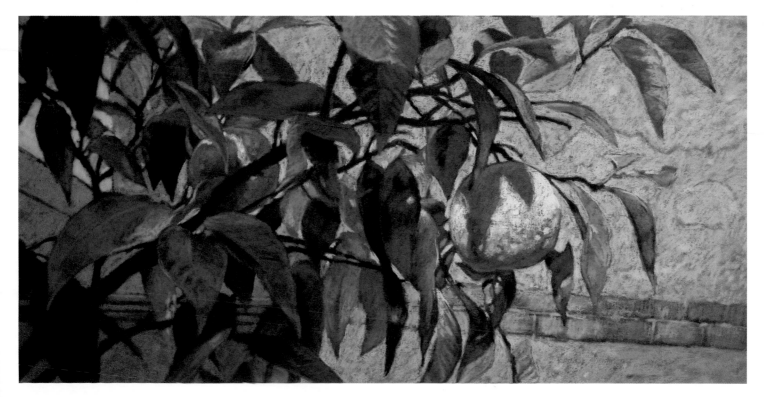

Light

Inevitably, when you work in colour and are dealing with the theme of landscape, you must engage with the effects of natural light. In some cases, this will be the very essence of your subject, for instance the charm of a particular view will stem mainly from such effects as dappled light under trees or the warm colours of afternoon light giving extra intensity to the landscape hues.

It can be hard to fix such transient effects when you are working on the spot, and photographs are not always good references as they may lose the colour clarity. Effective interpretation of light qualities comes in large measure from keen observation, but an equally important factor is confidence with your medium. Sometimes it helps to exaggerate contrasts of colour and tone and be bold and free in your mark-making – when you step back from the drawing, the individual elements magically cohere into a striking image.

A coloured ground is a useful starting point if you are trying to capture brilliant qualities of light. A base colour allows pale tints to stand out fully, whereas when you use white paper its own brilliance is constantly competing with the colours that you apply.

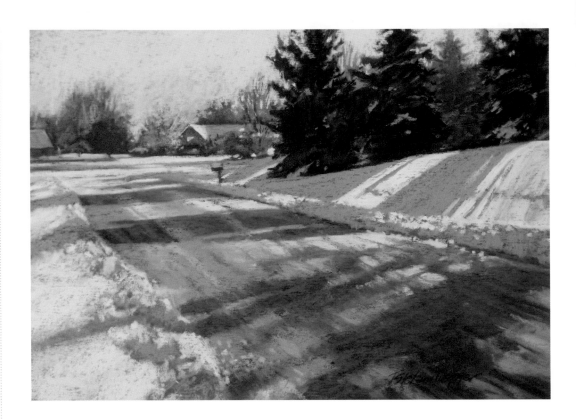

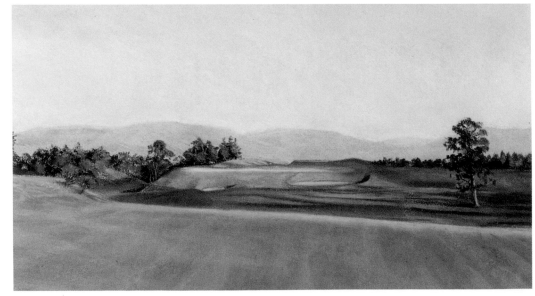

▶ JILL STEFANI WAGNER
ROGER'S FARM 1
Excluding the top of the large tree in the top right corner imparts a degree of tension to what might otherwise be a fairly static scene. The long shadows cast by the trees and the hint of pink in the sky just above the horizon suggest that this is either early morning or evening.

◀ JILL STEFANI WAGNER
AFTER THE SNOW
This image was done on blue pastel paper, so the brilliant white of the snow really stands out. The blue ground also sets the cool overall mood. Although it's a tranquil, peaceful scene, the composition is dynamic: the strong diagonal line of the road leads up to the houses in the distance; the shadows form more diagonal lines that are almost at right angles to the road.

◀ MARGARET EVANS
EVENING LIGHT, KING'S COURSE, GLENEAGLES
The lush green fairways of a well-kept golf course reflect the warm evening glow as distinct bands of golden light. There is a gentle gradation from cool greys and blues in foreground and sky towards the rich, warm yellows and ochres spread across the centre of the landscape.

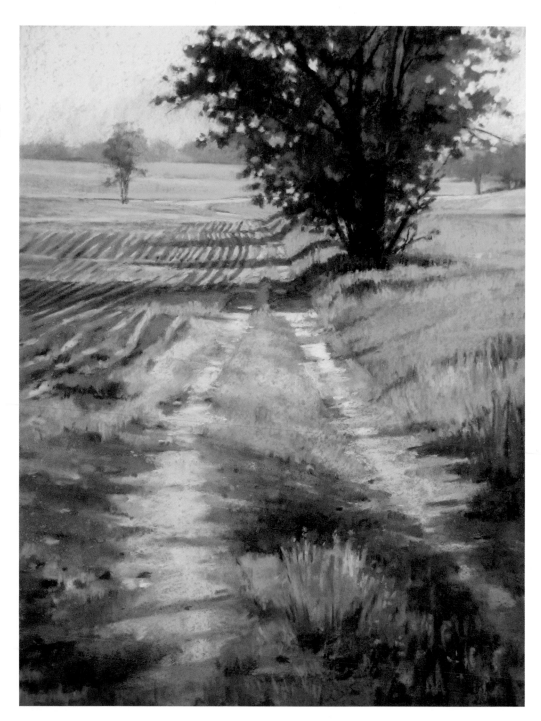

Skies

The most problematic aspect of painting skies is that the sky itself is largely composed of light, which you must translate into the colour equivalents provided by a solid, material medium. How you deal with this in terms of technique partly depends on the overall style of your image. Sky composed of many individual marks building up into a complex feathered texture or mass of broken colour can be surprisingly effective, but if the sky becomes much "busier" than the landscape it will begin to dominate the image and destroy the sense of space.

On the other hand, an evenly coloured, open sky may look too flat if treated over-simply. It might be advisable to use two or three closely related tints to give a little depth and variation, blending these if necessary to create a subtly coherent surface effect. Alternatively, you may wish to play up hints of colour or atmosphere, even giving the sky an unnatural colouring that expresses the mood of the image and forms an appropriate backdrop to the landscape subject.

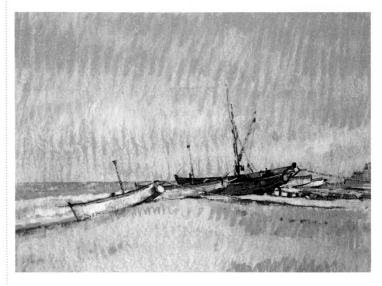

◀ **GEOFF MARSTERS**
LT229, IH88, IH265 AT ALDEBURGH
The colour nuances of a subdued, greying sky are developed with feathering of broad vertical strokes creating gentle gradations of the delicately varied tints. This vertical emphasis is repeated and emboldened in the treatment of the foreground plane, the two areas cut through by the strong horizontal arrangement of the boats. Their shapes are crisply defined with linear marks and clear contrasts of colour and tone that push back the evenly textured plane of the sky.

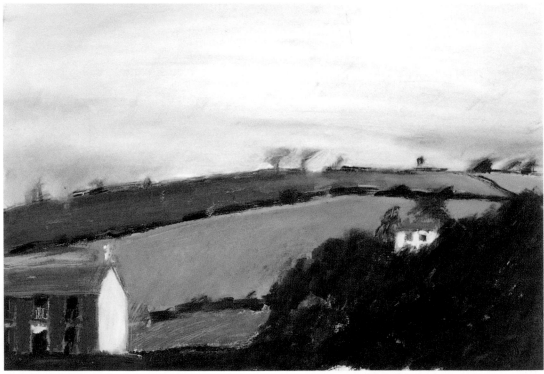

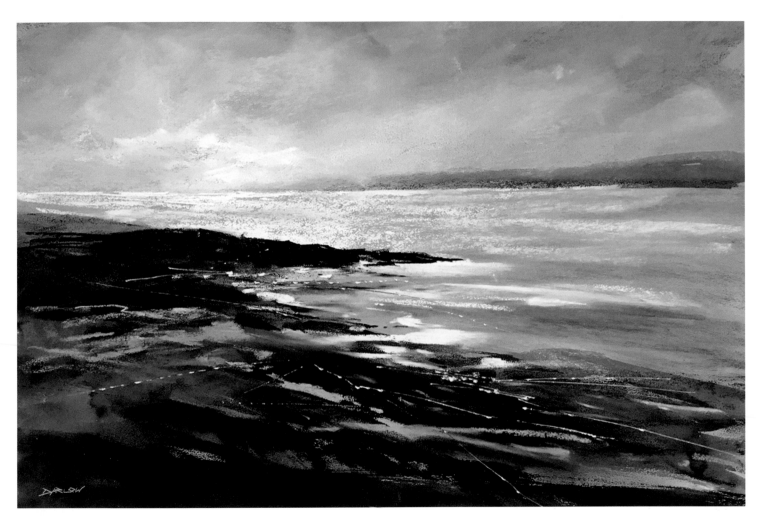

◀ JANE STROTHER
ONE WELSH HILLSIDE
Oil pastel and oil paint are
applied in layers, the pastel
moistened and spread with a
rag The technique provides
a veiled shadowing in the cold,
grey sky, its bleakness
counterpointed by glimpses
of a warm underlayer of red
on the horizon and in the
foreground.

▲ LES DARLOW
FADING LIGHT
Soft pastels are combined with
ink to great effect here, with the
inks giving solidity to the land
and the pastels being gently
blended to capture the subtle
colour changes in the sky. Note
how the tooth of the paper is
used to convey the effect of light
sparkling on the water.

Water

Streams, rivers, ponds and lakes are temptingly picturesque, and they also introduce additional elements of colour and texture that give pleasant variation to a landscape view. Clear water has no colour of its own, but "borrows" those of its surroundings in the form of reflections of sky or landscape features. Moving water has infinitely changing patterns of form, colour and texture, while still water can change from a flat, mirror-like surface to a complex mass of tiny ripples with the touch of a breeze.

Like skies, water can be interpreted in many different ways, and you can experiment with a variety of different technical solutions. However, because it has no fixed character, you need to pay careful attention to what you actually see in a given situation. Reflections can appear, for instance, either as a network of colours and abstract shapes or as a startlingly detailed, inverted picture of the landscape surrounding the watery surface.

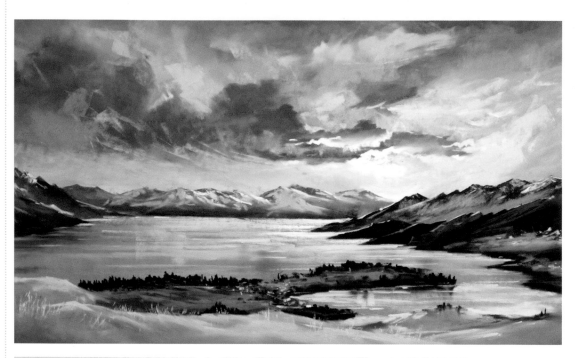

▲ LES DARLOW
THE REMARKABLES
The still waters of the lake reflect the colours of the evening sky and provide a calming counterbalance to the rolling clouds above.

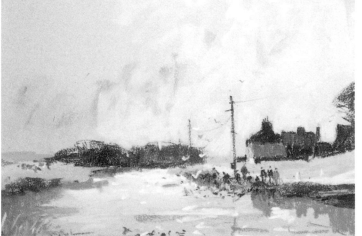

◄ JOHN TOOKEY
SALTHOUSE, NORFOLK
The water is described with definite strokes and pale, blued tints to indicate both its luminosity and the faint disturbance caused by its movement.

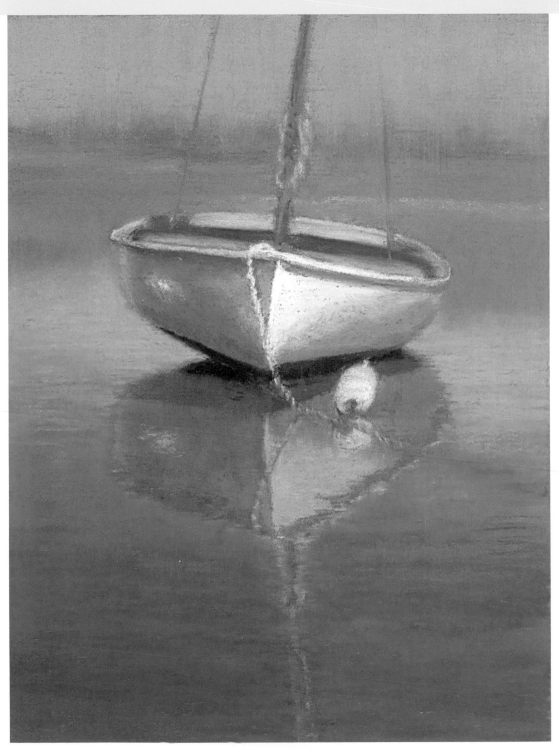

◀ **NANCY POUCHER**
CALM MORNING
A few very gentle ripples disturb the surface of the water, adding interest to what might otherwise be a featureless expanse. The background and the reflection of the boat were blended with foam pipe insulation, while the colours on the boat were not blended at all; this makes the reflection more muted in colour, separating it from the boat.

▶ **LYNDA CONLEY**
AUTUMN LAKE
Here, the spread of water draws
the eye towards the back of the
painting. There is a rich variety
in textures, notably in the
foreground, and overall the limited
palette creates a wonderful,
harmonious whole.

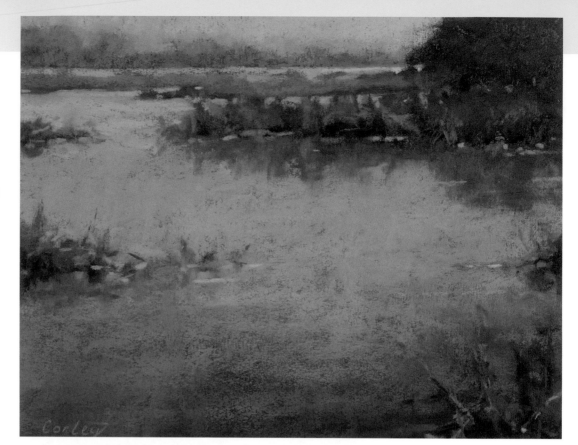

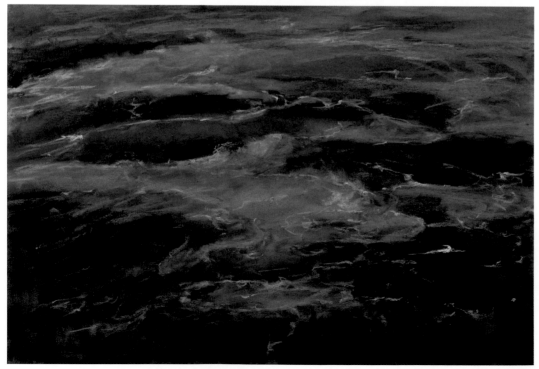

◀ **ENID WOOD**
SALT STREAM
Enid Wood's paintings usually
begin with one colour or an
unexpected pair of colours; the
rest of the painting takes shape
from that beginning. The vitality
of each stroke evokes a mood,
makes textures and creates
harmonies. Here the movement
of the water is beautifully
evoked with brisk strokes and
a combination of pastel sticks
with pan pastel.

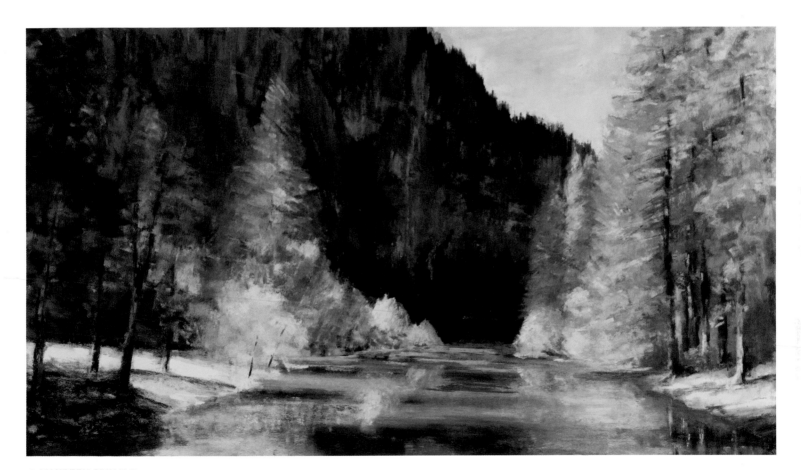

▲ MAUREEN SPINALE
THE WONDER OF IT ALL
The emerald green of the river, the strong light
and the majesty of the cliffs drew the artist to
this site. Maureen Spinale took several reference
photographs to document scenes in Yosemite.
First, the artist blocked in the large shapes with
stick pastels and then brushed with methylated
spirits. To this base, she applied layers of pastel.

Seascape

Seascape and marine painting are often seen as specialized subjects that individual artists will study and develop over a period of many years. The continual motion of the sea is both an inspiration and a difficulty; the latter because it disrupts the continuity of your observations and makes it hard to relate specific shapes, forms, textures and colour effects to each other and to the image as a whole. Good photographic reference may be helpful, but photographs do "solidify" the subject – a too hard-edged or static interpretation of the sea's rolling masses is a common fault of a beginner's efforts to get to grips with this awesome theme.

This problem is reduced if you are mainly interested in coastal landscape, when the sea becomes a background to other natural forms, and a certain static quality is not out of place. However, if you wish to incorporate effects such as lapping waves and rising spray, you need to settle for a period of trial and error until you become familiar with your subject's visual qualities and discover the most effective pastel techniques for representing them.

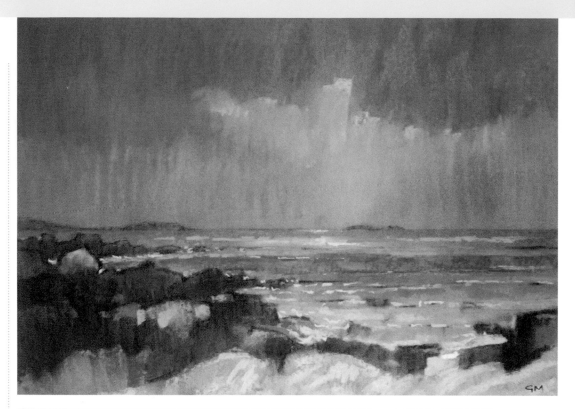

▲ GEOFF MARSTERS
BRETON COAST
The sky is always an important influence on seascape, and often a dominant area of the composition. Here the colours of sky and sea are closely linked, the change from vertical to horizontal stresses in the pastel marks emphasizing the spaciousness of the view.

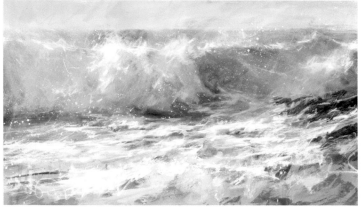

▲ JAMES BARTHOLOMEW
NANJIZEL BREAKER III
Combining watercolour and pastel, the artist has captured the energy and motion of the sea with energetic marks. The sky is reduced to just a small sliver at the top, focusing all our attention on the crashing breakers. The partially submerged rocks on the right help to give a sense of scale.

▶ LES DARLOW
BREAKING WAVES
There is incredible energy and movement in this scene, with the waves breaking over the foreground rocks in bursts and splashes of white. The glowering sky, underlit by the setting sun, imparts a warm glow to the whole scene.

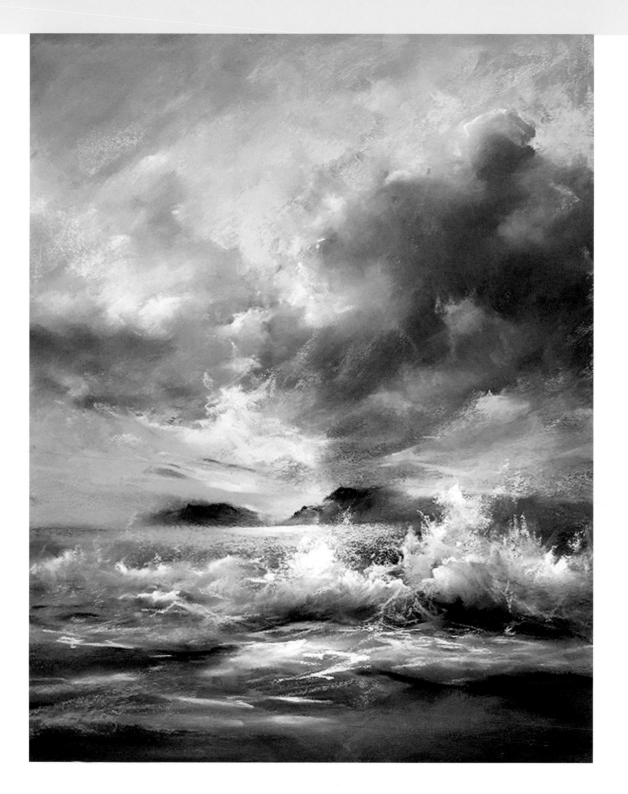

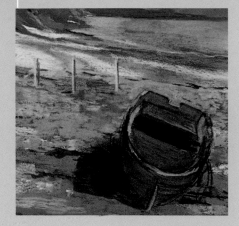

Demonstration

Hazel Harrison

The relatively simple construction of this composition emphasizes the sense of space. The soft pastel palette is effectively employed to recreate the atmospheric contrast of a dark, heavy sky and reflected light on the sand and stones of the beach.

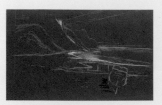

▲ **1** The composition's main features are sketched out in line. The blue paper is chosen to provide a dense background tone and to create an underlying colour contrast that will enhance the warm, sunlit colours of the beach.

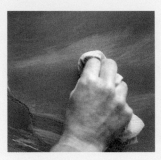

▲ **2** The lighter tones in the sky are freely shaded with the tip of the pastel, using pale grey-blue and cobalt. The marks are rubbed with a soft cloth to spread the powdery colour and form an atmospheric, hazy effect.

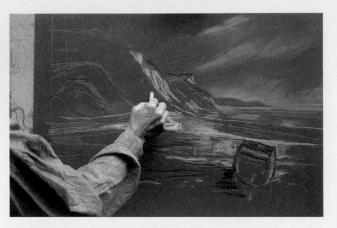

▲ **3** The artist continues blocking in the image with loose, rhythmic strokes, establishing the overall colour range more broadly and defining the structures of the main forms with line and mass.

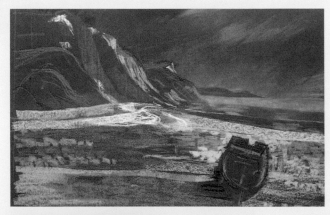

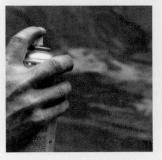

◀▲ **4, 5** Variations of colour and texture are developed in more detail with a combination of side strokes and linear marks. The contrast of cool colours in sea and sky and warm hues in the foreground enhances the spaciousness of the view. A light spray of fixative (left) is applied at this stage to seal the surface before reworking.

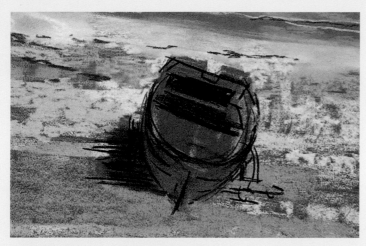

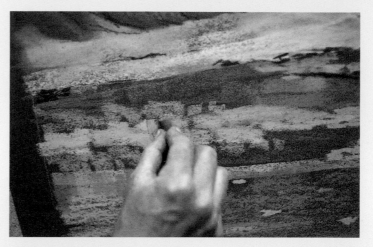

▲ **6** The artist continues overlaying colours to build up the landscape features. Corrections are made to the perspective of the boat, with the shape redrawn with firm outlines to redefine the structure and give it weight and depth.

▲ **7** In the final stages, the textures of the beach are elaborated. By introducing paler tints and increasing variation in the hues, the artist illuminates the foreground of the image, and emphasizes this by subtly greying the colours of sea and sky.

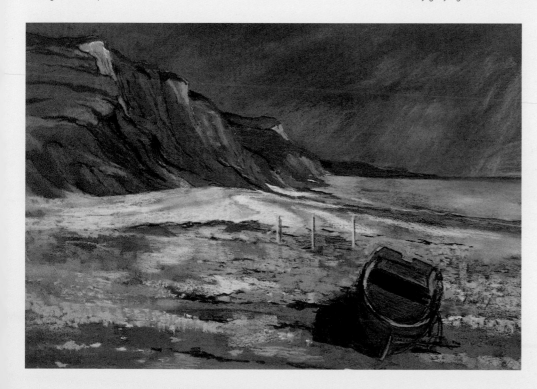

◀ HAZEL HARRISON
CHARMOUTH BEACH

Environment

The title of this section reflects the fact that themes in art overlap and defy strict categorization. All the images presented on the following pages relate to man-made aspects of the environment, but they frequently demonstrate a fusion of, for instance, elements of landscape and townscape, and present the ways particular locations form a context for human activity. Some of the artists have chosen to record their own immediate surroundings and picturesque locations.

Place and mood

Common to all is a keen sense of place, whether it is the individual character of a house or village, the detailed intimacy of a furnished interior, the bleak but familiar setting of an industrial townscape, or the colourful enticement of a busy market. Different aspects of the environment are interpreted in a range of varied and equally fascinating ways in this selection of paintings, sometimes highly realistic and descriptive, sometimes focusing more on mood and atmosphere.

A response to the mood of the subject is particularly noticeable here, but is similarly at work in many examples of other themes, particularly landscape compositions and works that feature figures, animals or objects in various settings. Technical factors can be descriptive not only of actual physical elements of your subject, but also of its broader character and the feelings you wish to convey.

Bold, active marks convey dynamic relationships of form and texture; softly broken or blended textures and broad spreads of colour are more gently atmospheric.

As you become confident of your technique, you can also become more ambitious in terms of composition. The way you present your subject can give it an emotional as well as material context: variations of style and technique can allow you to interpret a given situation as either welcoming and relaxed or mysterious and threatening. The extent and arrangement of the composition and the treatment of colours and tonal values convey your personal impression. Whenever you find an image particularly striking – its effect may be pleasant or unsettling – it should be possible to analyse some of the ways in which the artist has used technique and composition to create a mood.

▶ **AUDREY DULMES**
HILLSIDE HOUSES
Audrey Dulmes describes colour as her "muse" and here she uses a bold colour combination of oranges and greens. Both colours are shown in lots of different tones to give depth to the painting. Brisk mark making is used effectively to describe the landscape features.

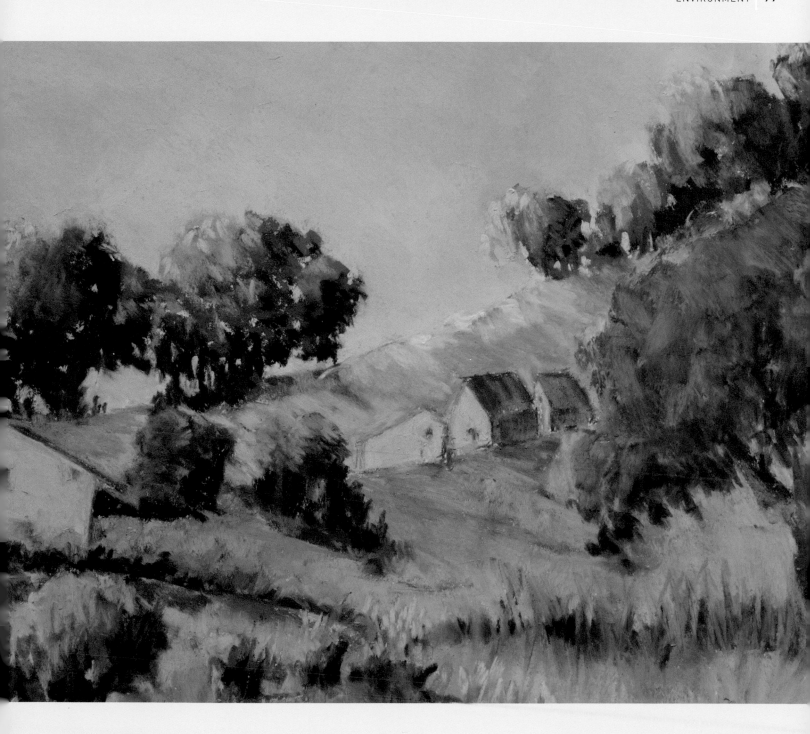

Buildings

The spatial organization of individual buildings and architectural groups often provides a ready made composition, with the colours and textures of the various construction materials adding surface interest. The colours and textures of pastels correspond well to features such as weathered brick, wood, stone and painted plasterwork. The medium's linear qualities also help to give definition to subjects composed of planes and angles.

A building often has a special character that makes it an attractive subject in itself. Its particular appeal can be stressed by the viewpoint that you take – distant or close, face-on or angled, with the building merging into or isolated from its surrounding context. The subject can also be enhanced by imaginative treatment of unusual effects of light and colour as well as basic physical attributes of shape, form and texture.

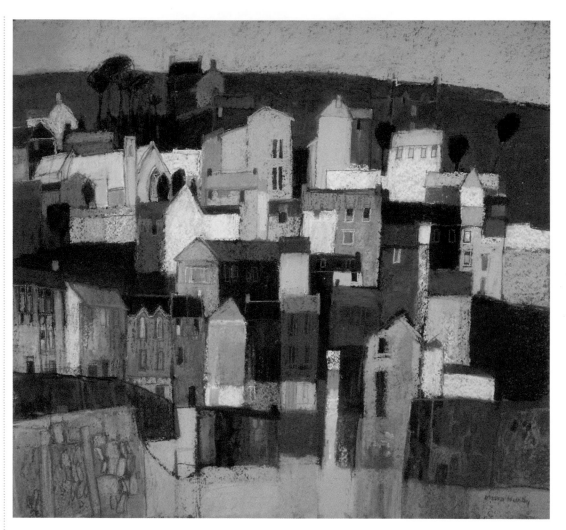

▲ MOIRA HUNTLEY
WATEFRONT BUILDINGS AT BRIXHAM
This painting is balanced between realism and abstraction. Although the buildings are portrayed as blocks of colour, the setting is recognizably that of a waterfront: the harbour wall (bottom left) and reflections in the water make this very clear. It is a kaleidoscope of shapes and colour masses.

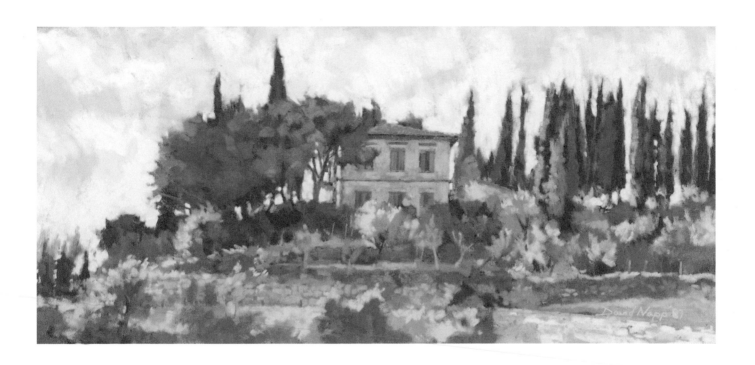

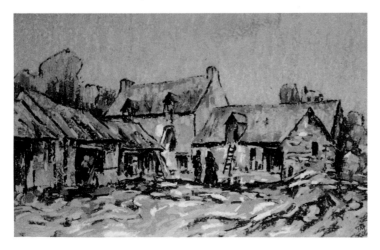

▲ DAVID NAPP
**HOUSE AND CYPRESS TREES
AT REGELLO**
The house is given a kind of
grandeur by its location, as the
arrangement of the composition
makes clear. The low-key
vibrance of the colours reflects
a serene mood.

◄ GEOFF MARSTERS
BRETON FARM
In this bold treatment, strong
outlines contain schematic colour
areas and textures, ranging from
foreground impasto to light
feathering in the sky.

Streets and Markets

Views of a town or village street are often most interesting as a setting for human activity. There is a fascinating contrast between the solid permanence of an architectural background and the colour and motion of people going about their business. The introduction of the figures enhances the sense of scale; the buildings may form a neutral backdrop to the human interest or may interact with and enclose them, depending on the viewpoint you take and the way you integrate different elements of the composition.

Street markets, colourful and containing a wealth of varied detail, are particularly fascinating subjects for drawing and painting. They exist in all areas of the world but are characteristically expressive of their own culture and community. They combine aspects of architectural, figure and still life composition and the vital interplay of moving and fixed forms.

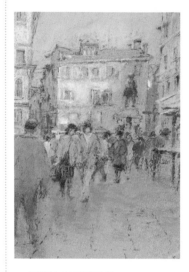

▲ DIANA ARMFIELD
MARKET STALL, PIAZZA BARTOLOMEO
The cast shadow of the right-hand building gives this composition a predominantly cool cast, against which the sunlit corner of the far building stands out dramatically. Both architecture and figures are described with a subtle interplay of free linear marks that structure the forms and areas of shading and broken colour that give weight and solidity.

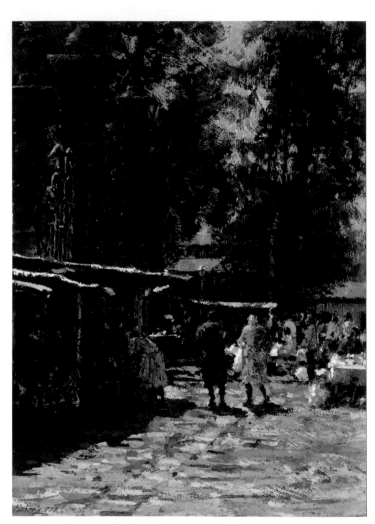

▲ ERIC MICHAELS
SUNDAY MORNING IN PATZCUARO
Here the artist makes full use of pastel's pure, intense hues, overlaying its grainy textures on the heavily contrasted pools of light and shadow created by a watercolour underpainting.

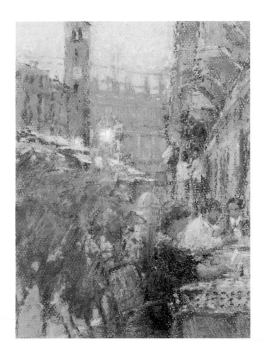

▲ DIANA ARMFIELD
AT THE RESTAURANT PIAZZA ERBE, VERONA
The foreground elements have been used to frame the view of the more distant buildings. The heavy grain of the paper contributes to the atmospheric effect of broken colour.

▶ JILL STEFANI WAGNER
VICOLO DEL PINO
Quiet alleyways tucked away from the crowds can just as effective as the more obvious tourist sites in evoking a sense of place. Here, the strong shadows and warm sunlight on the terracotta-coloured building on the right immediately mark this out as being a Mediterranean scene.

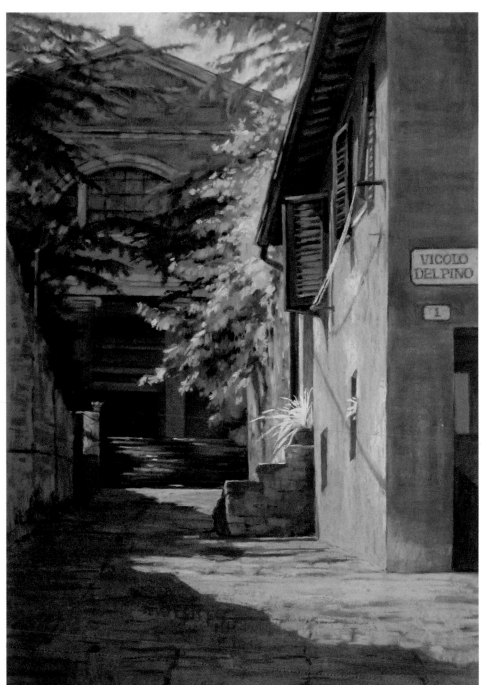

Industrial Settings

There is typically a kind of harshness to an urban industrial setting or working environment. Such subjects may not immediately present themselves as sympathetic vehicles for pastel work, but as the examples here show, pastel can be a tough, dramatic medium as much as it is a colourful and picturesque one.

Much of the interest of such subjects lies in the unusual configurations of shape and form presented by the various structures that play their part in a particular function, including buildings, machinery and vehicles. Linear frameworks and striking tonal contrasts are good material for a pastel rendering, and a subject that at first seems lacking in colour will gradually yield many subtleties of hue and tone. Some subjects have a stark, abstract quality that can be exploited in a broadly imaginative, interpretive vein.

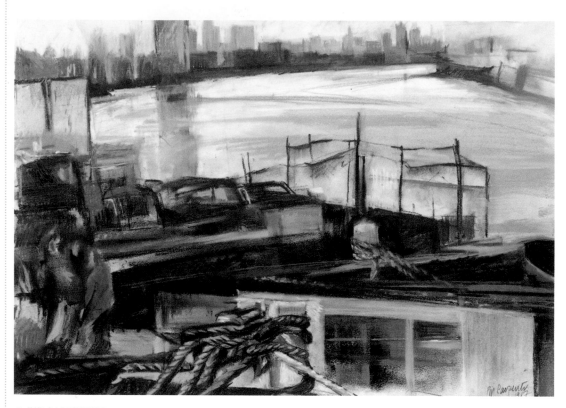

▲ PIP CARPENTER
WOOD WHARF BOATYARD, UPSTREAM
The texture of hard pastel is well suited to the geometry of the subject, and the artist finds plenty of incidental colour among the cold greys of the riverscape. The glassy surface of the river is represented with bold horizontal strokes in pure white.

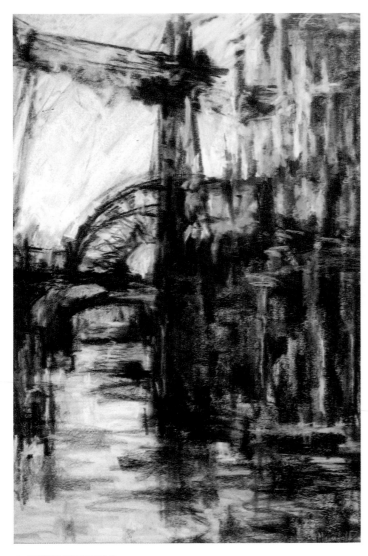

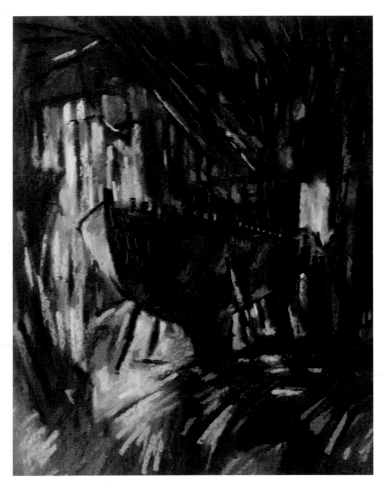

▲ DEBRA MANIFOLD
DOCKHEAD
To emphasize the stark drama
of the derelict site, colours are
limited to black and white with
occasional punctuations of green
and red. The drawing is rapid
and spontaneous, using a
combination of charcoal, oil
pastel and soft pastel.

▲ GEOFF MARSTERS
INTERIOR OF BOATHOUSE
The strong contrast of light and
shadow is constructed not only
with extreme tonal variations
but also with the contrast of
complementary colours. The
brilliant flashes of orange and blue
enhance the spatial organization of
shapes and volumes.

Interiors

The domestic interior is one of the most accessible subjects, indeed it is sometimes overlooked for this very reason – it is over-familiar. But the most ordinary room reveals a complex arrangement of forms in space and a wealth of incidental detail in the décor, furnishings and objects. If you use your own home as a subject, you can work very privately and at your own pace. As with still life, this is an opportunity to try out varied approaches and study different aspects of the subject at leisure.

Public settings such as a café or restaurant or the interior of a museum or place of worship are of interest both for their general atmosphere and for the specific details of purpose-built interior architecture. Perhaps there may be elaborate ornamentation, and formal organization of objects within the space.

Lighting is an important part of the mood and style of an interior. When working in a domestic setting you may wish to set up artificial lighting in a way that emphasizes space and structure, but it is often worth taking advantage of the accidental qualities of natural light. Strongly angled sunlight entering the window can create scintillating colour accents and dramatic shadows.

Sometimes you can see beyond the enclosed space of the room, through the window or into an adjoining room or passage, for instance. This adds depth to the image and may provide interesting contrasts of colour, light and texture.

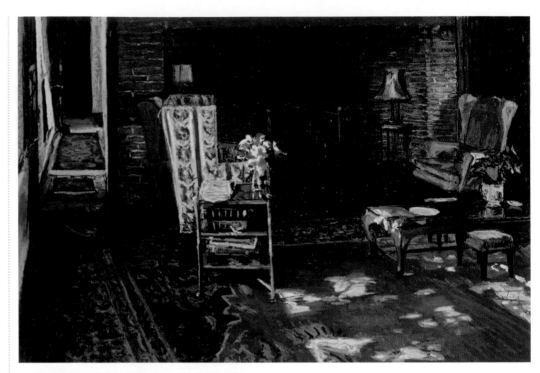

▲ MARGARET GLASS
THE PARLOUR, BALE
The pattern elements within the room are freely interpreted with decisive strokes building complex detail.

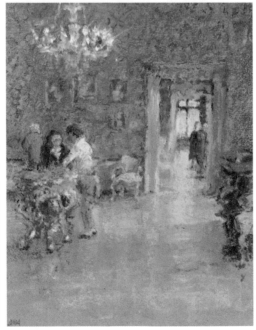

◄ DIANA ARMFIELD
IN THE CA'REZZONICO, VENICE
Like the previous composition, this image opens out the interior space by showing the view through into the rooms beyond. The pattern detail is softly worked with loose scumbling, its warm colours creating an agreeable contrast with the cool tints describing reflected light on the polished floor.

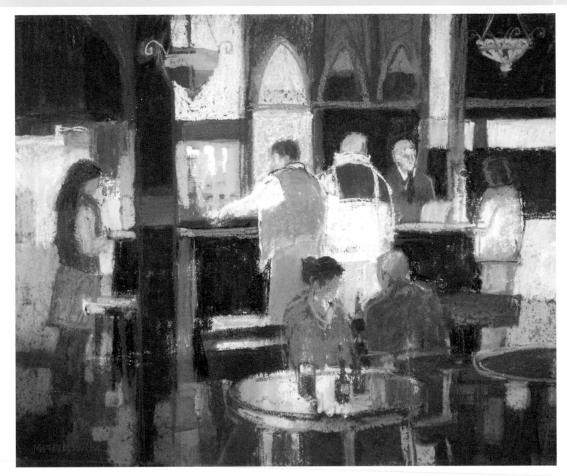

▶ MOIRA HUNTLY
O'NEILL'S BAR
The figures in this semi-abstract
scene are carefully framed within
the arches of the bar or set against
solid areas of colour. The
predominantly warm tones are
balanced by smaller patches of
cool blues and whites. The pillar
on the left divides the composition.

▶ CHARLOTTE ARDIZZONE
INTERIOR WITH SOFA
Vigorous hatching and
crosshatching, varying the
directions of the pastel strokes
constructs the planes of the
interior and objects within it. The
high-key palette of colours gives
a vivid quality of illumination.

▶▶ TOM COATES
INTERIOR WITH SEATED FIGURE
The monochrome scheme and
open, sketchy style of this drawing
dispense with details of colour and
texture but precisely construct the
space and scale of the room.

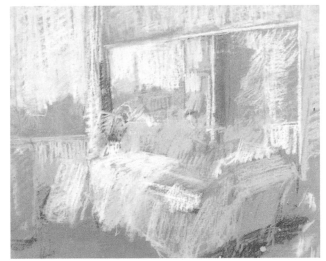

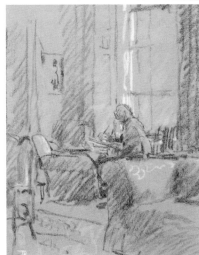

Mood and Atmosphere

A sense of mood derives from a complex interaction of factors, from simple physical characteristics to memories and associations brought to an image by artist or viewer.

Some places have an inherent atmosphere relating to their appearance or function; some present a different character according to the weather or time of day. A straightforward record of a particular environment may in itself convey a mood, but you can also take a more deliberate approach and use formal elements of drawing and painting, such as colour and composition, to develop your feeling for a subject and communicate more than just an immediate visual impression.

Your viewpoint and the extent and organization of your composition contribute to the mood of the subject. An individual building or a whole town can be made to appear isolated and remote by placing it centrally within a broader landscape. A low-level or flatly frontal view makes the building seem less accessible than an angled, eye-level view that emphasizes ways into and around the structure.

Harsh lighting or exaggerated colours can create a sense of alienation, while naturalistic colour, even with strong lights and shadows, is more reassuring. Colours and their tonal values are often associated with mood, and although personal responses to colours vary, there are some reliable general rules. For example, neutrals and pastel colours are more serene than pure, bright hues, and gentle gradations of tone similarly create less impact than strong contrasts of light and dark.

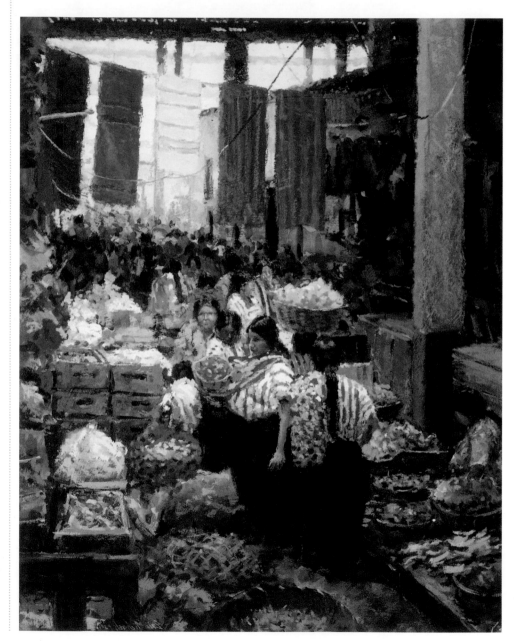

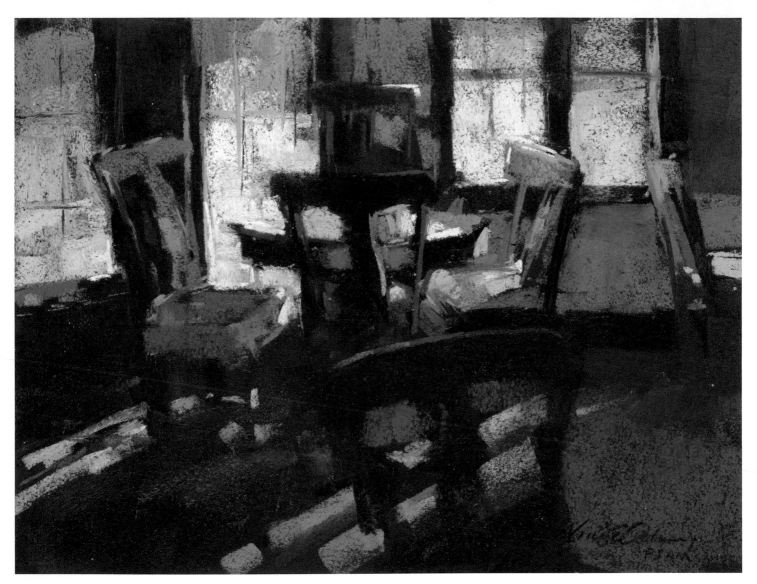

◀ ERIC MICHAELS
INDOOR MARKET, SANTIAGO
The busy atmosphere of the
market is encompassed in the
long view of the market hall,
which allows so many elements
of the activity to be seen. The
composition was first blocked
in with watercolour, then
developed with an intricate
build-up of pastel marks.

▲ ALINE E. ORDMAN
CHAIRS
The lightly scumbled colours on the
window panes create a lovely sense
of light, as do the shafts of light
reflected on the floor. This contrasts
with the heavier applications of
pastel on the chairs.

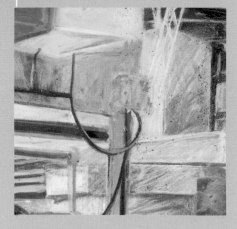

Demonstration

David Ferry

The solid geometric volumes and intricate structures of an industrial construction site are colourfully described in this image, in which the artist employs an inventive mixed-media approach to develop different qualities of form and surface texture.

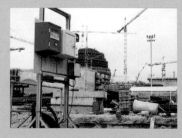

▲ **1** The large-scale construction site incorporates a complex interaction of organized structures and randomly placed elements. The artist needs to deal with the variety of shapes quite selectively to avoid overcomplicating the image with indistinct features.

▶ **2** A good-quality printmaking paper is pinned to the drawing board and the image area framed with strips of masking tape. As the techniques to be used will involve wetting the paper, it has to be heavy enough to resist buckling. The basic shapes within the composition are drawn freely with a 2B pencil.

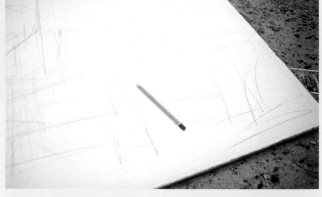

▶ **3** Aerosol spray paints, of the type sold for retouching the bodywork of automobiles, are sprayed on the paper to form a loose underlay of background colour. This method is chosen as a quick way to give an overall balance to the initial pencil line drawing.

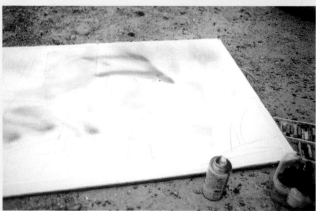

▶ **4** The separate planes of the main structures are blocked in with broad hatching in oil pastel. Coarsely spattered colour is also applied by flicking ink from the bristles of a brush.

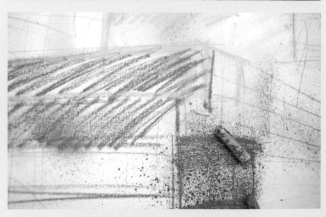

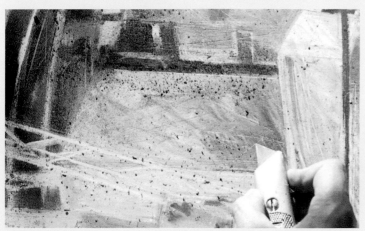

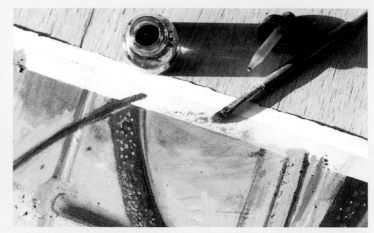

▲ **5** The artist gradually builds up the planes and volumes with broadly textured areas of oil pastel colour. Firm impasto strokes are used to develop linear structures. The colours are freely blended and overlaid, some areas reworked as sgraffito, using a craft-knife blade to scratch into the surface layers and increase the range of textures. A stencil brush has also been used in places to "mash" colours together and roughen the surface.

▼ **6** The geometric qualities of individual shapes are more sharply defined, with the edge of the pastel used to draw strong, heavy lines, sometimes guided by a ruler. In this picture, you can also see areas where the artist has used stippling and scraping out to vary the surface qualities of the pastel marks, and where the slight translucency of oil pastel has been exploited in creating depth in the colour overlays.

▲ **7** Coloured ink is brushed over the pastel, intensifying the brightness of the hues and introducing a rhythmic brushed texture. The artist can work freely over the edges of the painting, as the masking tape protects the borders of the paper and will ensure that the final image is cleanly framed.

▼ **8** The area of sky that forms the background of the image is also reworked with fluid ink washes and spattering applied over the oil pastel marks. This use of resist technique creates a very rich texture which the artist develops with soft, stabbing strokes of the brush. Here again, the masking tape is forming a clean edge to the rendering over which the brushwork can be freely manipulated.

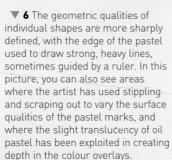

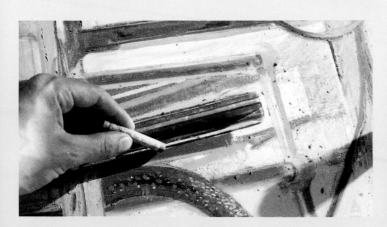

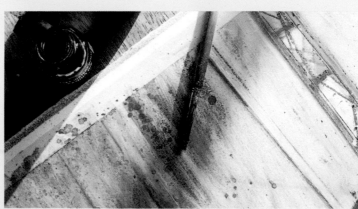

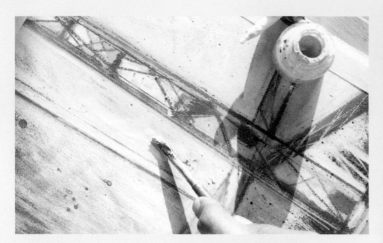

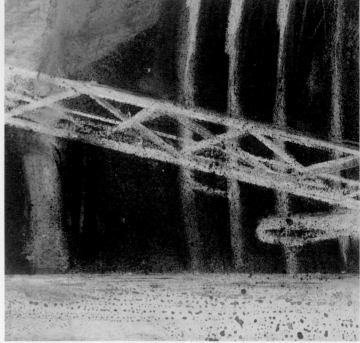

▲ **9** The artist now uses opaque white ink to "tidy up" areas of the drawing and block out any loose pastel marks that he does not wish to keep. This heightens the pale tone of the sky behind the crane tower, throwing its linear framework into sharper relief.

▼ **10** When the artist is satisfied with the balance and detail of the rendering, he removes the masking tape that frames the picture area. Despite the vigorous activity of the ink and pastel work within the frame, the masking has maintained a firm, hard edge, an important element in the overall image.

▶ **Mixed media effects**
These details of the finished picture show the immense variety of surface texture obtained by the different techniques, particularly the fluid patterning of ink and oil pastel resist (top left) and the harsh, calligraphic quality of sgraffito (left). The artist has also made the most of individual colour cues, such as the strong red of the oil drum, and has enlivened the image by interpreting the industrial greys with loose colour mixes of yellow, brown, purple and blue.

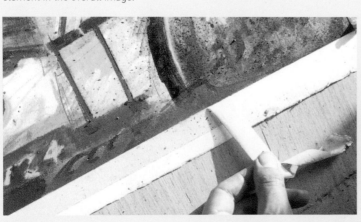

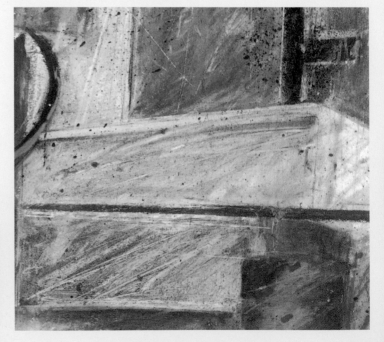

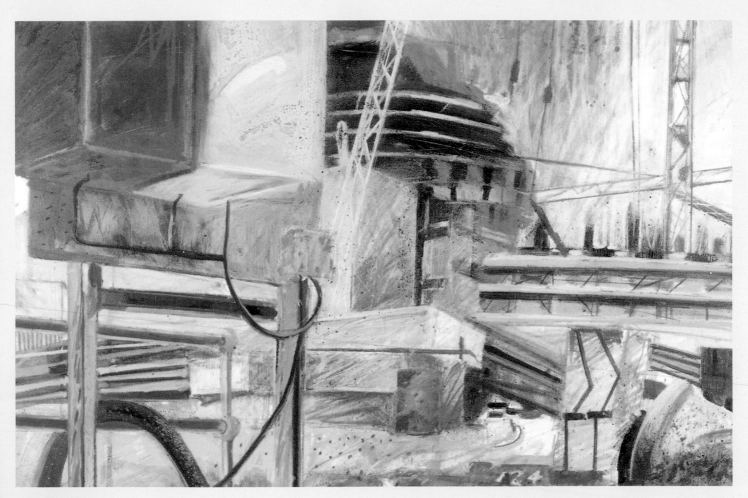

▲ DAVID FERRY
CONSTRUCTION SITE

The Figure

The human figure is an extensive resource for the artist, providing a theme that encompasses many different formal and expressive elements. You can view a figure simply as a compact structure composed of related forms and volumes, or you can engage with the individual person, so that your rendering identifies a particular mood or activity or locates the figure in context by details of dress, accessories and environment.

The many different traditions of figure work give artists all kinds of access to the subject. Study of the nude figure has been a classic element of formal art training for centuries and many artists still feel it is an important aspect of figure work, hence the survival of the traditional life class. For most of us, however, the theme of the human figure comes in terms of ordinary people – people that we know, people that we see in the course of daily life. Among the most accessible models are family and friends, often seen at home and engaged in everyday activities. To avoid formal posing you can catch these subjects while they are relaxing – reading, watching television, listening to music, or even asleep.

Beyond these domestic situations, you must begin to accommodate more movement in the figures, as with people you see in the street or park. If you wish to make movement a more prominent element you can go to locations where activity is the main purpose – such as a sports centre or dance studio.

The medium

Pastel is a very versatile medium for figure work, as the images you create can vary from quick sketches to highly finished, detailed, full-colour compositions. Pastel's linear qualities can express contour, direction and motion, while its painterly ones provide the means to interpret mass and colour.

Your approach to figure work and the techniques that you use depend to some extent on your viewpoint and the figure's prominence in the overall composition. Because of the directness of pastels, you need to have a sense of what most interests you about your subject so that you can develop your work to the desired stage without too much overworking or correction that might deaden the image. Your technical skills need to be subtly varied if you are working on close studies, where nuances of tone and texture make a dramatic contribution to the finished image. On the other hand, if you are drawing a crowd of figures in a busy shopping street or recreation area, a single pastel stroke may represent a whole head or torso, giving the general impression of individual figures emerging from a mass of brief marks and colour accents.

▶ SALLY STRAND
COURT BREAK
This artist achieves a remarkably precise sense of realism, yet the images are large and her technique allows a great deal of freedom. She first draws in charcoal on heavy watercolour paper, then rapidly brushes, in watercolour washes to define basic shapes and forms. These washes are the opposite colours of what the pastel painting will be – for example she lays in warm ochre for an area that will ultimately be blue. The pastel overlays are built up with linear marks, working from dark to light and counterpointing the hues and tones. In later stages, side strokes and finger blending add to the weight and solidity of the forms. The quality of light is orchestrated by means of colour. There is no white in this painting – the players' clothing is a brilliant combination of pale tints, including green, blue, mauve, pink and yellow.

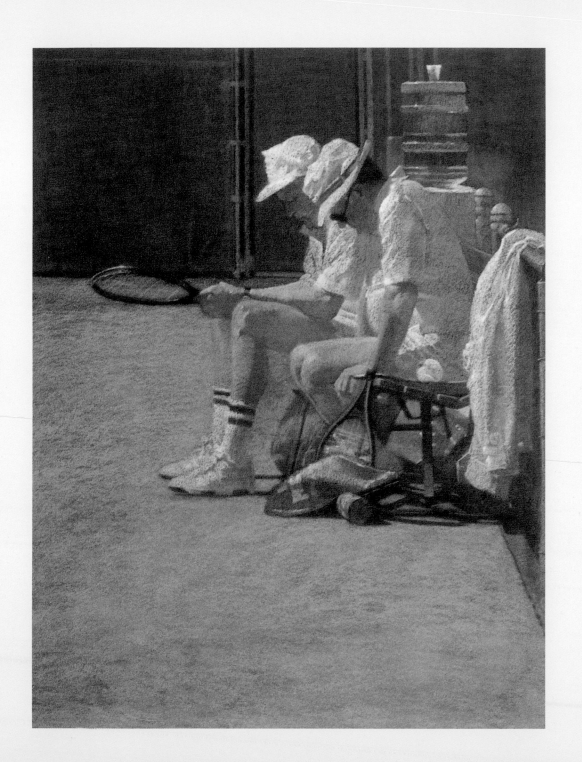

Standing Figures

The standing figure is a dynamic form, the body seen in full proportion and with the tension of imminent movement — since few people stand stock still for long. Every standing pose has its own specifics of weight and balance, for instance the torso may be firmly supported on both legs, or have the weight shifted to one side with one leg bent or extended. Other factors that contribute to the balance of the pose are the angle of the head in relation to the body, and the disposition of the arms.

The individual character of the figure in a particular pose is a combination of internal and external detail. The simple outline of a figure can be very telling, but the volumes of which it is composed, and their formal relationships, create the solid sense of realism.

Clothing adds colour to your rendering, and is also expressive of both form and character. It makes useful surface detail, but look for the ways in which it can also describe aspects of the pose, emphasizing or concealing the contours of the body and adding to the rhythms and tensions of the figure.

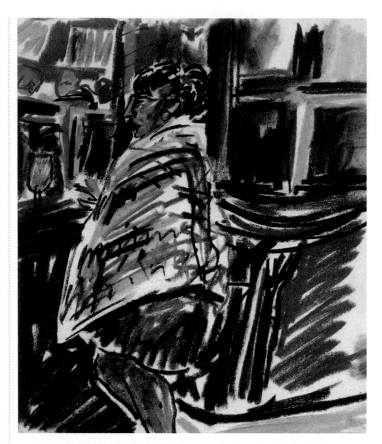

◀ IRENE WISE
SYLVIE AT THE PARIS RENDEZVOUS
Vigorous gestural drawing creates a bold image capturing the mood and character of the subject. The contours of the figure are simply expressed, but are finely descriptive of the body's weight and balance.

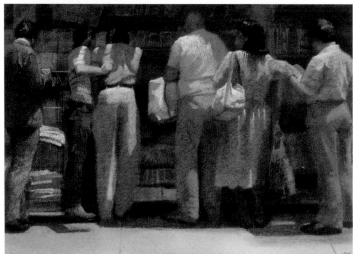

◀ SALLY STRAND
CORNER OF 48TH
This neatly aligned figure group incorporates subtle but very dynamic shifts in the poses. Notice the solidly vertical stance of the man on the right, the slight backward angle of the woman beside him and, in turn, the forward-leaning attitude of the man in front of her.

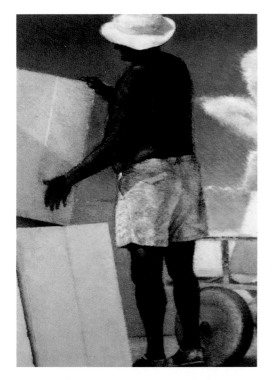

◀ **KEITH BOWEN**
SPANISH QUARRY
(DETAIL)
The stocky shape of the stoneworker is seen as a virtual silhouette against the pale tones of the sky and stone, but each component is subtly modelled with light and shadow. The tilt of the body is seen in the repetitive, parallel stresses through the shoulders, waist and alignment of the feet.

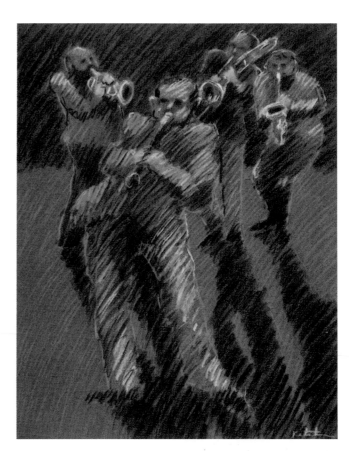

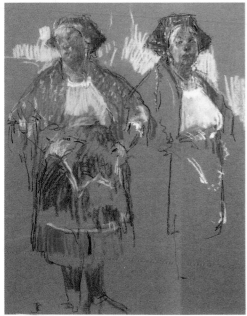

◀ **TOM COATES**
PEASANT WOMAN
The solidity of the figure emerges clearly from an outline sketched in black and loosely filled with colour. This is a very stable pose, the axis of the body running vertically and balanced by the angles of the arms.

▲ **CAROLE KATCHEN**
PEANUTS HUCKO
Although the body shapes are not precisely realistic, they are wonderfully expressive of the musicians' energy and tension, the active qualities of each pose enhanced by the loose hatching of the pastel strokes.

The Figure in Action

The study of a person performing a specific task may be an opportunity to portray an unusual configuration of body and limbs and to examine visual rhythms and tensions not expressed in formal poses. There are different ways of conveying activity and movement, the two most common being, a "freeze-frame" approach that focuses one aspect of the action, and the more abstract, sketchy approach often applied to rapidly moving figures.

Examples of the latter method are illustrated in the following section, while the compositions shown here take the first approach, a "snapshot" of the figure at work or play. In portraying the figure itself, it is important to notice the exact angle and direction of different parts of the body which contribute to the action, and also the way clothing and props help to explain the activity. Each of these images is carefully composed to convey the impression of the person's physical and mental concentration.

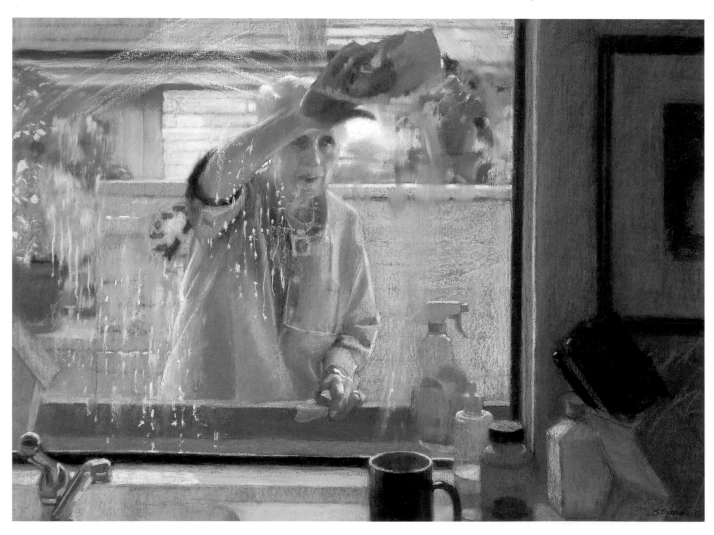

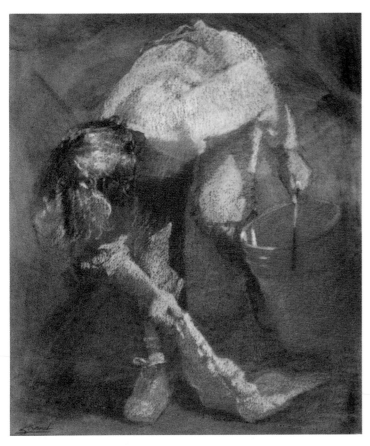

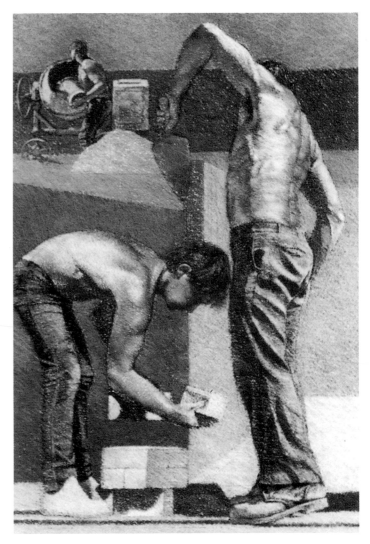

▲ SALLY STRAND
NEARLY OVERLOOKED
The action is described both by
the contour of the body and the
pattern of light and shade within
it, the rhythms, echoed by
directional strokes.

◀ SALLY STRAND
WINDOW
Everyday tasks provide you with
the challenge of portraying the
commonplace in a compelling way.
Here the pose and the rivulets of
water running down the window
create a lovely sense of movement.
Including some of the kitchen
interior provides an insight into
the subject's domestic life.

▶ KEITH BOWEN
BRICKLAYING
The bent and stretched poses
of the bodies create an active
configuration offset by the
geometry of the location.

Movement

Very rapid motion is difficult to convey, although as previous examples have demonstrated, precise rendering of a split-second action can be highly descriptive, seeming to encompass the essential character of the action. A very different approach is taken here, using the calligraphic qualities of the medium and the free motions of the hand to travel along with the whole movement, building up a dense network of related marks and overlapping contours. This is particularly effective with stylized or repeated movements, such as dancing or exercising, as certain visual cues and points of reference return throughout the cycle.

This needs a vigorous, uninhibited technique — the drawing should emerge quite freely. There is always an element of experiment and some sketches will be more successful than others, but as you will be working rapidly you should soon achieve some interesting results.

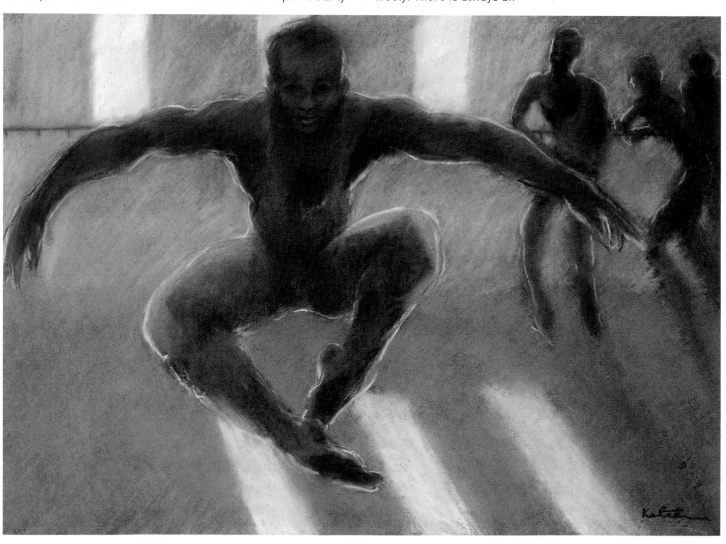

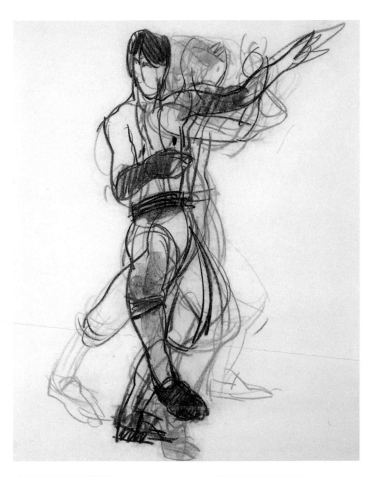

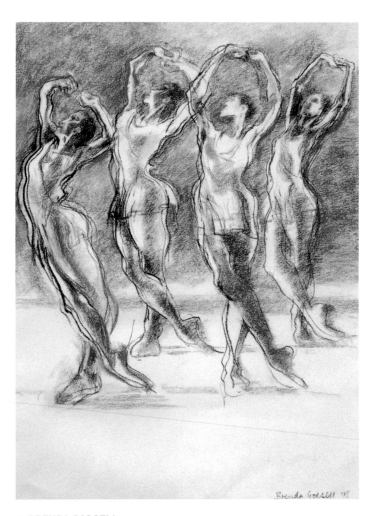

◀ **CAROLE KATCHEN**
RONNIE IN THE AIR
Loose shading and colour blending produce a soft sfumato effect which is highly atmospheric, but the slight dissolution of the figures is pulled back by the brilliantly lit, broken contour lines. The painting is quite large, 75×99.2cm (29½×39in.), so that the gestural qualities of the densely meshed strokes are clearly visible.

▲ **GEORGE CAYFORD**
T'AI CHI EXERCISE
When describing the continual motion of a figure, it is necessary to guide the pastel freely in direct response to the movements as they are seen. Speed is essential, thus the pastel is used here mainly as a line medium, with varying colours explaining different sequences of the exercise.

▲ **BRENDA GODSELL**
DANCERS IN GREY
In this charcoal and pastel study the tonal balances construct the figures quite solidly, but the rapid retracing of the contour lines contributes the fluidity and rhythm of transient poses that will shortly flow into different configurations. Because the colours of pastel are so appealing, its dramatic potential as a monochrome drawing medium is often overlooked.

Groups

Figure groups can represent all of the visual points of interest of the single figure, but their interactions are the keynote of the image. The elements of composition are as important as the details of individual form and character — alignment of the figures, the relationships of size and proportion, the space or closeness between them, and the relative distance from the viewer.

The grouping may be random, as with people on the street, or it may be due to a common purpose, of people come together to share an activity or form an audience. The active and passive relationships between the figures can be expressed in the composition, whether or not the group's full context and surroundings are portrayed.

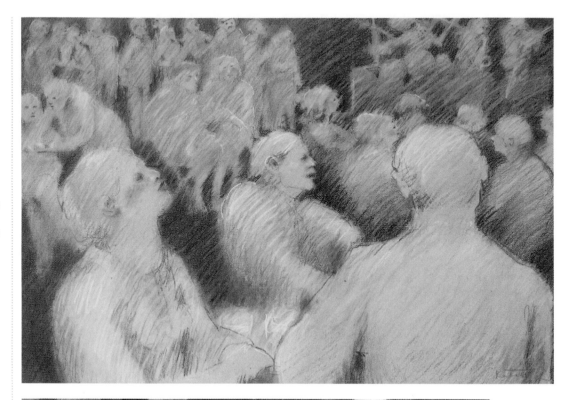

▶ SALLY STRAND
TAKING THE DAILY PAPER
The artist enjoys the incidental compositions of daily life. The extraordinary qualities of light and colour in her large-scale pastel paintings are built up gradually, playing off dark against light and warm colours against cool hues.

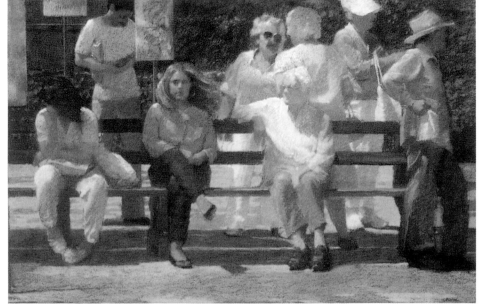

◀ CAROLE KATCHEN
JAZZ AT THE MUSEUM
The consistency of style and
technique in this composition
is employed in emphasizing
variations of form and character
in the informal figure group.
Individual body shapes and
poses are broadly conveyed,
but incorporate many subtle
nuances of form and direction.
The controlled colour scheme
effectively suggests a particular
quality of interior light.

▶ ERIC MICHAELS
**AT THE WELL –
CHICHICASTENANGO**
The randomness of figure groups
that are "found" rather than posed
creates interesting compositional
elements. This close focus
on forms cut off by one another
and by the framing of the
composition creates an intriguing
sense of narrative as well as
a vivid orchestration of colour
and pattern.

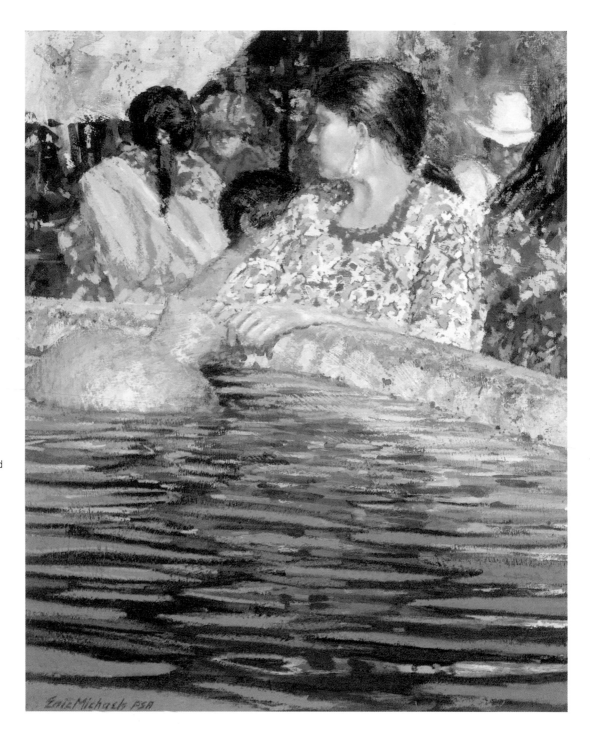

Children

The commonest problem in drawing children is identifying the precise characteristics that make them childlike – they are not mini-versions of adult people. The head is larger in proportion to the body than in the adult; the limbs are mobile and flexible, but the chubbiness typical of young children disguises bone and muscle structure.

Another difficulty is getting a child to pose. If you are working from life, you need to choose a style and technique that enable you to work quickly or can accommodate changes in the pose if the child becomes fidgety. If you are working on a more complex composition that needs prolonged attention to detail, you may need to work from photographic reference and, if possible, ask the child to pose briefly to check any elements of form and posture that are not clear from your reference pictures.

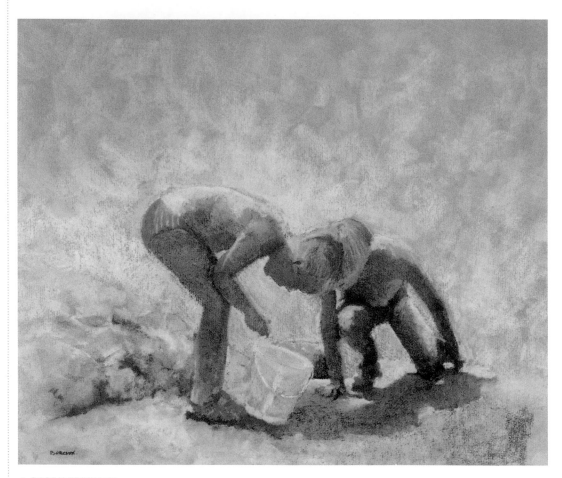

▲ BARRY FREEMAN
CURIOSITY
Children have an easy suppleness that enables them unconsciously to create graceful poses in the course of ordinary action and play. In this composition the two bodies are linked in a rhythmic, self-contained shape at the centre of the composition, the more striking because detail of their surroundings is minimized. The natural colour range and gentle technique express the simple pleasure of the subject. Broad, grainy pastel strokes juxtaposed and densely overlaid create defined areas of integrated light and colour.

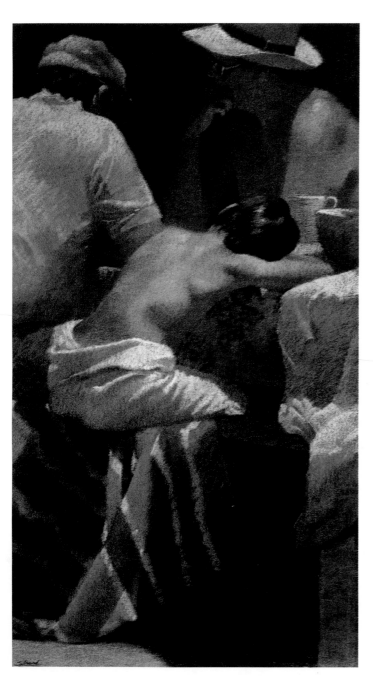

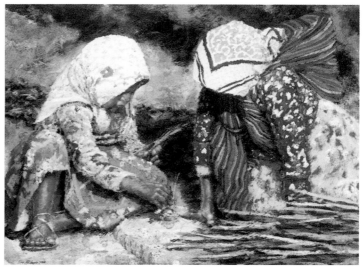

◀ SALLY STRAND
PLAYED OUT
This lyrical painting demonstrates that there is no particular trick to portraying children; it simply requires highly accurate observation. Here the artist has found the precise contour and texture of the child's body that are unmistakably expressive of his youthfulness.

▲ ERIC MICHAELS
SIMPLE TREASURES
Like the painting of the two boys on the beach opposite, this delightful study captures the typically childlike poses and concentration on play. The style of their bright clothing, introducing an exuberant colour range, appears imitative of the adult version, but the weight and proportions of the bodies and the tiny glimpse of the left-hand figure's face all display the characteristic features of the child.

Figures in a Setting

Many of the figure studies illustrated in this section show at least some of the surroundings. In some cases it is no more than a general indication of the kind of space the figure occupies, while in others the setting is treated in enough detail to suggest a kind of narrative background. Describing the setting can help you to explain the character or action of the figure, but it also expands the range of compositional elements that need to be considered from a technical point of view.

The more of the surroundings you include, the more you encounter the elements of scale and space. An interior setting introduces a specific perspective; a landscape background has to convey its space while sensibly relating to the size of the figures. New details of colour and surface texture are added to the composition, and as the figure becomes one of a number of visual components, you need to decide how to use your pastel techniques either to make the figure stand out as a focal point or to integrate it with the other elements.

There are various technical factors that you can bring into play here, such as the emphasis and activity of the pastel marks, and how these are used to describe different elements of form and surface detail. Other factors are the colour relationships within the image, with strong colours used as points of accent and focus; the patterns of light and shade that model the spaces and volumes; and the relative distinctness of individual shapes and forms, as when something that is sharply described stands out against a more impressionistic background.

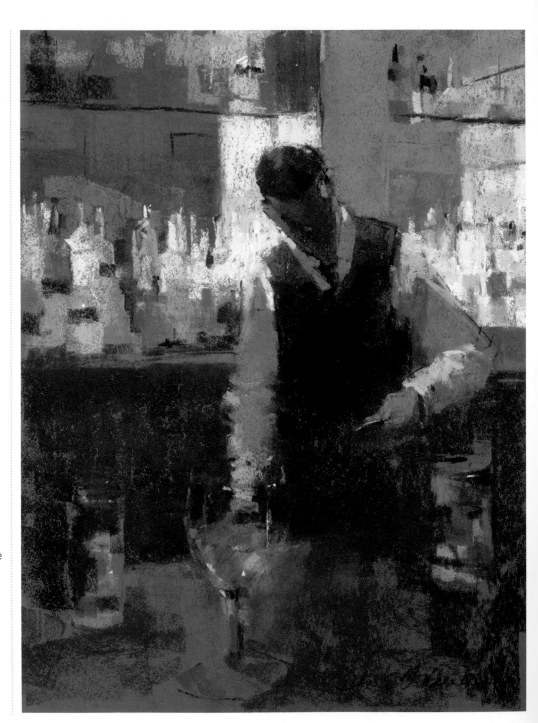

◀ ALINE E. ORDMAN
BARTENDER
In this work the setting, with the numerous glasses and bottles, is as important as the figure of the bartender – and pastels are wonderful for capturing the transparency of glassware and the way colours are reflected and refracted by it. Although we can't see the bartender's face in any detail, the balance of the pose – the tilt of the head in relation to the shoulders, the angle of the crooked arm – has been very carefully observed.

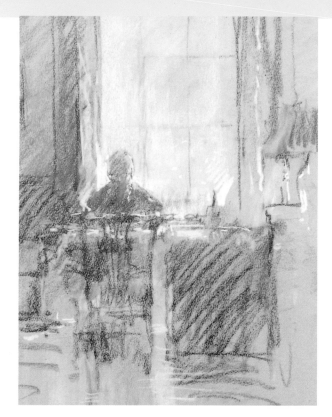

◀ TOM COATES
FIGURE AGAINST A WINDOW
A familiar domestic setting can become a powerful study of light and form. In the direct frontal view of the figure seated before the window, the composition is a bold construction of geometric planes and simple masses, economically drawn with monochrome lines and shading and enlivened with warm/cool colour accents and strong highlighting.

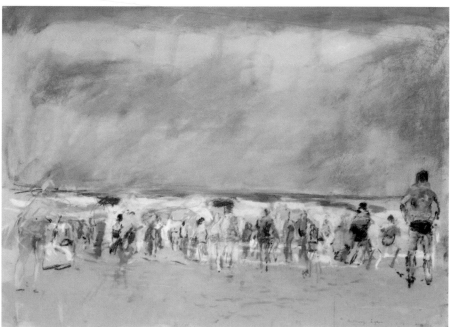

◀ ANTHONY EYTON
BIARRITZ
This is a rapidly executed study, with the main colour areas of sky, sea and beach freely shaded and scumbled and the dense activity of the figures applied gesturally, using linear marks and dashes of vivid and dark-toned hues.

Life Studies

The classical and academic values of the life class persist in that the unclothed human body is still used as a vehicle for studying form and proportion. However, with the enormous variety of technical and conceptual approaches that have emerged in the modern age, the nude study also remains an active inspiration. It can be treated purely as a drawing exercise, but is often interpreted more expressively; each example illustrated here conveys a different mood and context.

Outside the formal life class, it can be difficult to set up the right situation for this kind of figure study. But if you can find someone willing to pose for you at home, the more intimate atmosphere of a domestic setting gives an evocative character to the image. Nowhere is the formality of life drawing better integrated with a personal and social context than in Degas's pastel paintings of women bathing — and his inventiveness with technique and composition makes these images enduring models for pastel work.

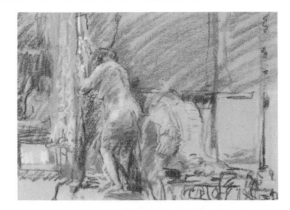

◀ TOM COATES
MODEL IN STUDIO
The broad setting of the life room is included in the composition, so the figure becomes only one element, not the main focus. Her attitude also suggests an incidental movement rather than a formal pose, which creates the logic of the sketchy technique applied to the drawing. The figure is differentiated by its form rather than by colour detail.

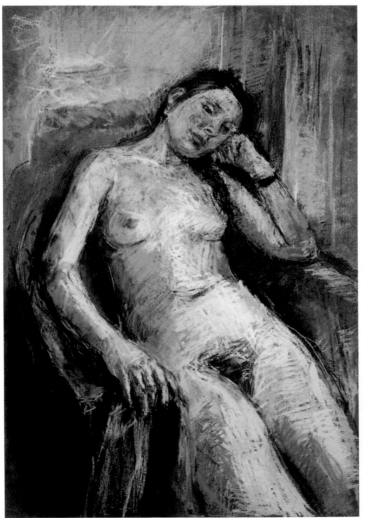

◀ ANTHONY EYTON
CRYSS IN A PINK CHAIR
This is a large painting, just under 1.2m (4ft) high, allowing the pastel strokes to display considerable energy right across the surface. The artist used fixative frequently throughout all stages of the painting, to help get the drawing right and create a ground to work on. It was drawn from life, requiring six or seven sittings to complete the image.

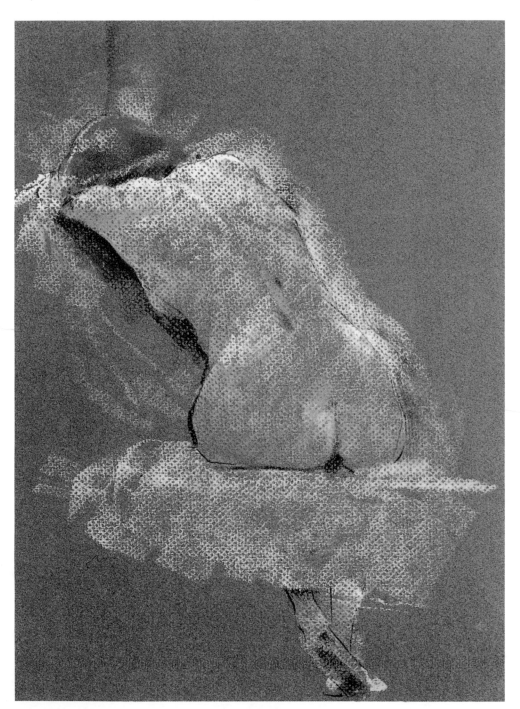

◄ **CLIFFORD HATTS**
A LIFE STUDY
The contour of the figure is sharply drawn with hard pastel, the delicate colours brushed in with gentle side strokes in soft pastel. The heavy grain of the textured ground breaks up the density of the pastel, providing a basic mid-tone that accentuates the hints of strong colour and gives the tints and highlights a special shimmering vibrance.

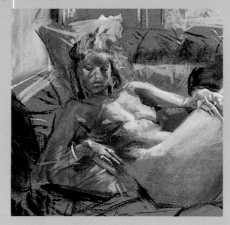

Demonstration

Vincent Parker

The classical reclining pose is adapted to a distinctively modern setting. The window provides strong directional lighting, and the artist uses both the figure's natural flesh tones and the primary colours of the cushions to illuminate the image with pure hues and brilliant pale tints.

▶ **1** The dense grey-blue tone of the paper will give additional vibrance to the pale, warm flesh tints. A simple line sketch in black establishes the main volumes of the figure and the specific angles of the pose. The artist uses bright pastel colours to dash in a few strong lines and grainy side strokes that form an initial key for the colour values.

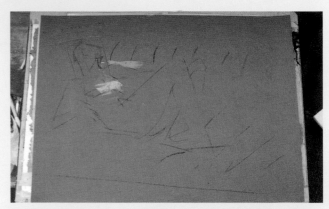

▶ **2** A general impression of the light and mid-tones is blocked in with side strokes and roughly blended colour areas. The colour blocks are complemented by active linear marks relating to the contours and angles of individual forms. Notice how the artist has begun to set up links between similar values of hue and tone across the whole image.

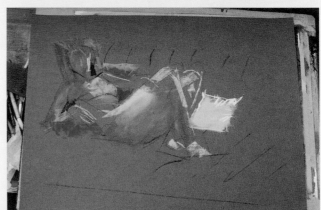

▶ **3** Bold line work is used to retrace the contours of the figure, complemented by broad, grainy side strokes to block in shadow tones that emphasize the volumes. The use of black and dark brown against the high yellows creates a vibrant tonal contrast, enhanced by the complementary colour of the blue ground.

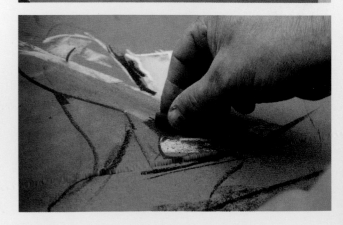

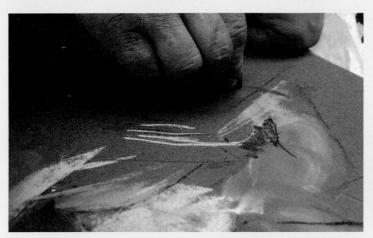

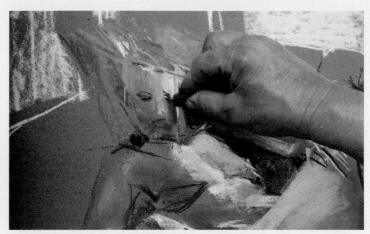

▲ **4** Within the limited scale of the drawing, the artist uses a free, gestural approach, forming active marks and a variety of surface qualities. He moves easily between drawing with the tip of the pastel to blocking in broadly with side strokes, rubbing the colours in places to produce loosely blended masses. To limit the scale of the marks, small broken pieces of pastel are used for the side strokes.

▼ **5** By this stage the figure has firmly taken shape. Dark contours are contrasted with intense highlighting in white. The light from the window is suggested by the simple block of white shading, which relieves the uniformity of the background tone. By sketching in the sofa, the artist sets the figure fully in context.

▲ **6** Individual features of the body and head are developed in more detail, combining strong, structural line work with solid colour masses creating volume. To model the forms, the artist uses not only dark tones but also cold, pale hues that suggest shadowing by contrast with the warm brown and yellow flesh tints. Frequent accenting with vivid hues keeps the surface alive.

▼ **7** Although the head is quite a small element of the image, the linear marks are laid in freely and boldly to structure the details of face and hair. The colours and tonal values are also boldly stated, seeking a distinctive impression of form and texture before more detail work is done to refine the shapes.

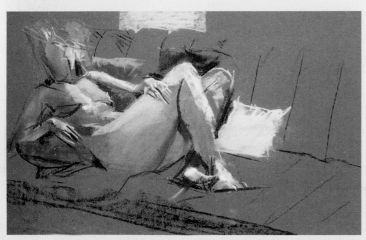

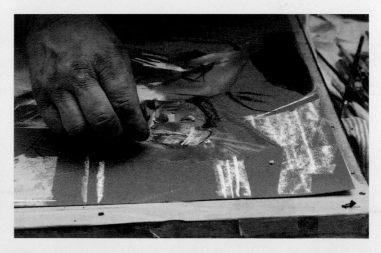

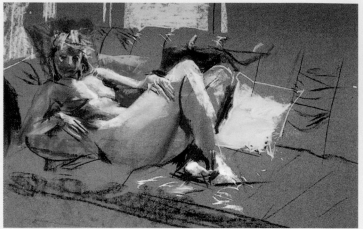

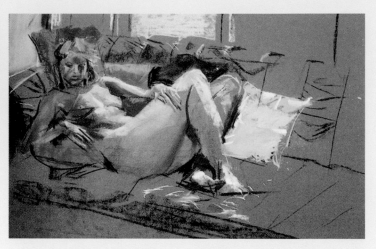

▲ **8** Many elements of the image are still very open and sketchy, but the rendering already conveys a clear sense of the interior's spatial arrangement and of how the weight and volume of the figure are solidly supported by the sofa and cushions. The many individual pastel marks have a great sense of vitality, but their interactions contribute to an increasingly subtle representation of form.

▼ **9** The face and hair are reworked with vigorous hatching, the linear pastel strokes smudged and dragged with the fingers to build up the density of colour. Although there is a random element to this kind of free technique, the artist is paying careful attention to the resulting qualities of tone and texture.

▲ **10** The solid volumes of the sofa and cushions are more fully described, enhancing the tonal contrasts to create a more vivid sense of illumination. The blacks loosely blocked in with side strokes are underpinned by heavy line work, and a similar technique is applied to the dramatic bright yellows of the right-hand cushion.

▼ **11** This detail gives an interesting impression of the virtually abstract pattern of individual marks and shapes that the artist is building, yet each element has a specific function in developing the structure of the image. Parts of the surface are still grainy, juxtaposed with areas where the colours are richly blended and overlaid.

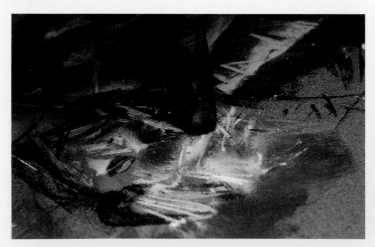

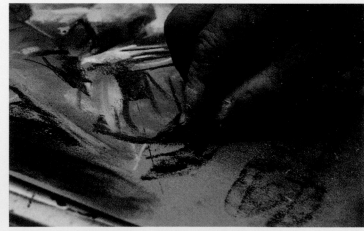

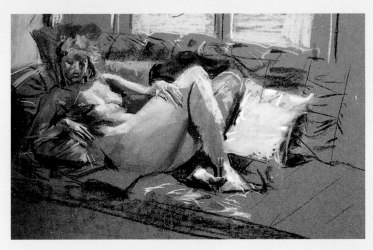

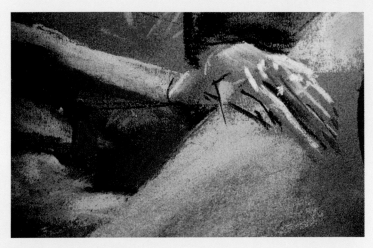

▲ **12** With the second windowpane sketched in with loose shading, the tonal balance of the image is adjusted once again. The artist rapidly dashes in brilliant colour accents with short, slashing strokes to heighten the strong hues of the blue and green cushions.

▲ **13** In the final stages, the artist concentrates on bringing up the highlights, adding touches of pure white to the hands and, face and brightening the pink cushion behind the model's head (see below). Although many details of the form are not rounded out fully, the finished image is both highly descriptive and vividly expressive.

▶ VINCENT PARKER
RECLINING NUDE

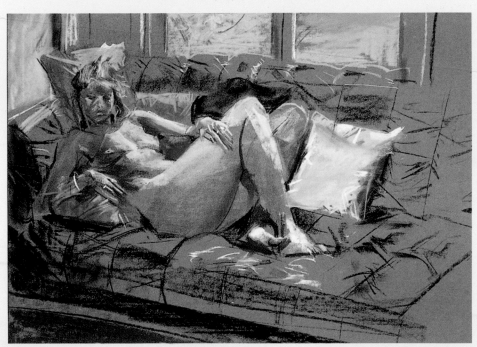

Portraits

Portraiture is one of the classic themes of pastel painting, richly expressed in the work of 18th-century artists such as Rosalba Carriera (1674–1757), Maurice Quentin de la Tour (1704–1788) and Jean-Baptiste Perronneau (1715–1783). It was carried through into the modern age by artists as diverse as Henri de Toulouse-Lautrec (1864–1901) and Umberto Boccioni (1882–1916). Whereas the earlier artists took advantage of the smooth blending qualities and subtle tints of soft pastels to produce detailed, complex portrayals of facial features and lavishly styled accessories, their modern counterparts exploited the medium's expressive qualities of brilliant colour and linear vitality.

The likeness

Portraits take many forms and involve different degrees of visual analysis, but their essence lies in creating a likeness. This does not necessarily mean accurate "copying" of a person's features — sometimes the detail of the features is indistinct, or even absent, but the character of that person emerges vividly from minimal visual cues.

The best portraits contain something about the mood and style of the sitter. It may pay you to risk slight exaggeration of the most dominant features, to emphasize the person's colouring, to pose them in a way that demonstrates an unusual but characteristic gesture. You can also select clothing, props and background that give the subject a particular context, and provide you with additional formal elements of composition that you can work with inventively.

One of the difficulties of portraiture is persuading someone to pose — being an artist's model is quite boring, and often more of a physical strain than you anticipate. You can work up a successful portrait from a photograph — in fact, an ordinary snapshot can be the inspiration for a drawn or painted portrait, because candid photographs often capture a transient expression or mood that represents the person more effectively than a static pose.

When you work from life, it is not necessary to condemn your model to hours of immobility; for one thing, tiny shifts in the pose and changes you incorporate when coming back to work after a break can give vitality to the image. Because pastel techniques have such immediacy, you should be able to establish a good grounding for the portrait in a relatively short time. Both the theme and the medium call for an approach that maintains its freshness and spontaneity — a series of quick colour sketches is a good build up to a full-scale rendering. Portraiture is not best served by laboured technique.

▶ SALLY STRIDE
ERICK
This is a charming character study, although details of the facial features are deliberately vague. The shapes of head, body and limbs and the overall posture are highly descriptive. The relatively simple colour treatment of the figure throws him into relief against the complex masses of pattern and texture in the surrounding interior setting. Clean, sharp highlighting adds to the definition of form. The colour range is richly varied but effectively balanced, giving full impact to the individual hues and tones, but adding up to a cohesive, expressive image.

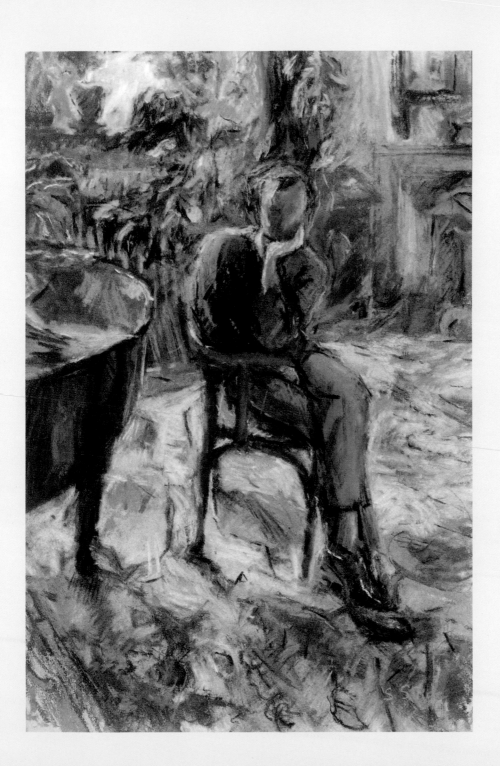

Heads

The face is usually the focal area of a portrait, so it is common that pastel portraits concentrate on the head. This single aspect of the person presents many challenges to the artist — the shapes of individual features are crucial, as are the colours of the skin tones and the way the hair frames the face.

The details and nuances are small scale and require very concentrated attention. However, they do not necessarily have to be tightly drawn to achieve the likeness; they can be very successfully represented using vigorous strokes and a bold approach to line and mass.

Facial features — eyes, noses and mouths — are difficult to draw. While some artists have a happy facility to catch the precise shape and form with a few brief marks, others find these details extremely troublesome and fail to marry observation and technique. You need to study carefully the precise shapes and apparent outlines of the features, the way they are modelled with subtle shifts of light and shadow, the tiny colour changes that give life to eyes and mouths.

Skin tones vary enormously, both in their natural colouring and with the kind of light thrown on the face. In pastel work it is common to use broken colour effects rather than smooth blends to model the contours of the face, because in this way you can pick up and make the most of every colour detail. As demonstrated in the examples here, if you work on coloured paper (see Coloured Grounds, page 12), it can be left bare or lightly covered to represent the base colour of the skin or the shadow colour. This is a helpful technical aspect of the pastel portrait.

Hair is a part of the portrait you can have fun with when using pastel, the linear quality of the pastel strokes lending itself to the textural detail. This can be contrasted with the techniques used to portray the face, or it can be integrated with the strokes describing flesh tones and shadows.

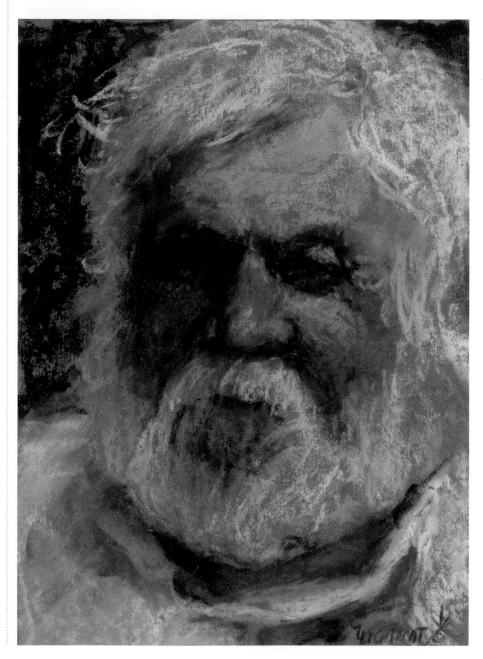

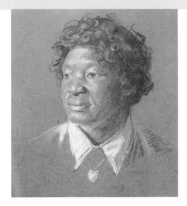

▲ JOHN HOUSER
AMANDA OF JOHN'S ISLAND
The colour of the ground forms
the basic mid-tone of the skin,
the lights and shadows colourfully
interpreted by hatching and
crosshatching. Shadow lines
around the eyes, nose and chin
are strengthened with unexpected
touches of pale blue and bright
red rather than conventional
dark tones.

▶ MARK DEMSTEADER
CIPRIANA
This portrait combines pastel and
collage and started with a tonal
drawing using black and white
pastels. The artist then threw
water over the pastels to create
drips and smudges that he could
work into, and finally tore up bits
of paper to make the collage.
Although perhaps not evident at
first glance, the collage hints at
the bone structure and breaks up
the flat, two-dimensional surface
of the image.

◀ LUVERNE LIGHTFOOT
SHADES OF GREY
Here, soft pastels have been
applied over hard to create a
subtle portrait that is full of
character. The shock of white hair
is drawn with confident, vigorous
strokes and stands out well
against the dark green
background.

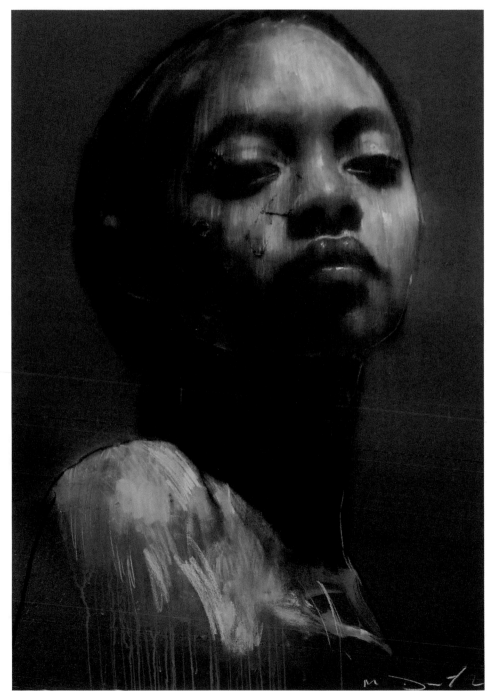

Age and Character

The age of the model is a fascinating aspect of portraiture, because different stages of life are represented by different kinds of visual information. The most obvious is skin texture — young skin is typically smooth with fresh colouring; ageing brings character lines and wrinkles, stronger shadowing of the features, and skin tones that are weathered or faded.

Other important cues are contained in the structure of the face, the shape of the head and the posture of the sitter. In children's faces the features occupy a relatively small proportion of the whole head, and details are unformed. In adulthood the underlying structure of bone and muscle shapes the face, and individual features become strongly defined — a heavy jawline or prominent nose, for instance. With age the patterns shift again, eyes and mouth perhaps becoming sunken, skin more heavily folded, and the hairline receding, altering the proportions of face and head.

The attitude of the head can also be characteristic of age and personality. A direct frontal view suggests confidence and maturity, a downward or sideways tilt can imply youthful diffidence.

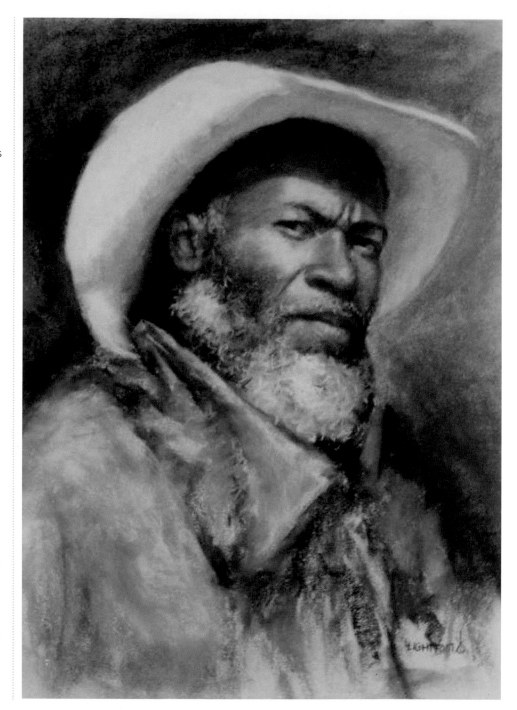

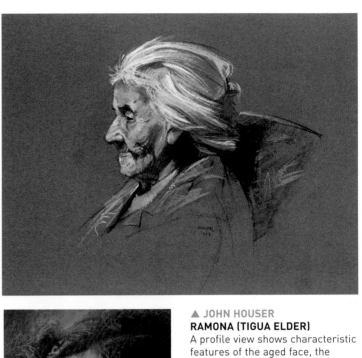

▼ JOHN-FRANÇOIS LE SAINT
MORGANE
The fresh skin tones of the young
girl are achieved by blending layer
after layer of colour, with the detail
added at the end.

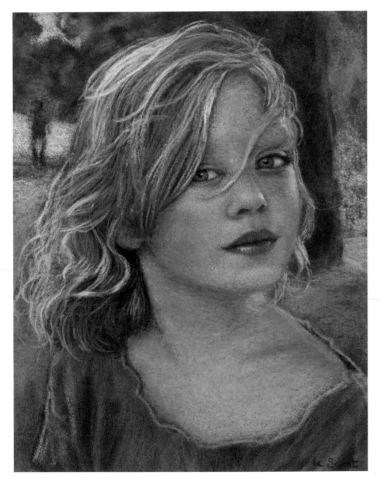

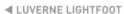

◄ LUVERNE LIGHTFOOT
TIMPANI
The model's slightly furrowed brow and direct
gaze are somewhat confrontational, and the
viewpoint – looking down at us – reinforces this
feeling of dominance. The background is reduced
to an impressionistic blur of colour, in tones similar
to but darker than those in the subject's clothing, so
that it doesn't distract from the portrait.

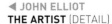

▲ JOHN HOUSER
RAMONA (TIGUA ELDER)
A profile view shows characteristic
features of the aged face, the
sunken eyes and mouth giving
prominence to the strong lines
of nose and chin. Skin tones and
shadows are built up with a
complex network of linear marks
and shading. The warm colours
and pale tints stand out on the
deep blue ground emphasizing
the modelling of the profile.

◄ JOHN ELLIOT
THE ARTIST (DETAIL)
This portrait has a fascinating
ambiguity: the eye is immediately
taken by the patriarchal white
beard before registering that this
is attached to a face not yet aged.
In the beard and hair the basic
colours are loosely laid in with a
form of scumbling, then developed
with a complex pattern of brief,
vigorous linear marks. In the face,
the hatched and shaded colours
are more closely integrated, giving
the firm profile an imposing,
sculptural quality.

Full-length Portaits

The more of the model you include in the portrait, the more elements you can bring in to round out the description. The posture of the sitter, for instance, can express something about his or her character, hands convey a lot about age and lifestyle, and clothing and background can suggest occupation and interests. You may, of course, ignore these aspects and concentrate on the formal aspects of figure drawing.

When you set up a full-length portrait, think carefully about the relationship of composition and technique. Consider how prominent the figure should be within the overall image and the scale of the rendering. Decide what it is that really interests you and relate it to the techniques you wish to employ. A free approach can work on either a small or a large scale, the pastel marks being highly interactive if tightly contained, and more open and gestural on a large scale.

Bear in mind that if you include a lot of props and background detail that you wish to describe with some precision, the actual execution of the work will take some time.

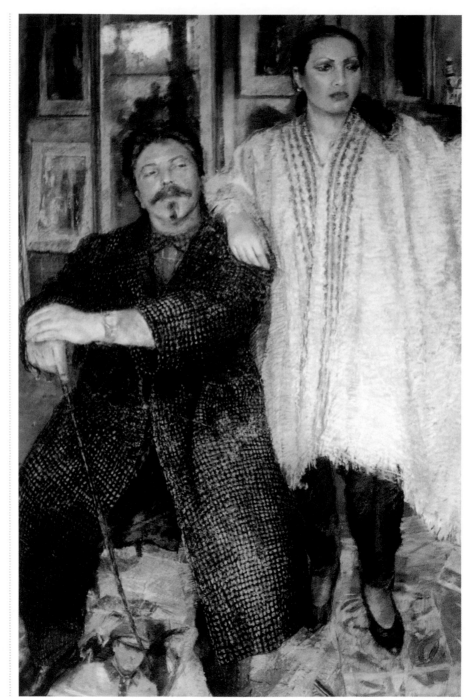

◀ **BARRY ATHERTON**
UNFINISHED
At 2.1×1.5m (7×5ft) this is unusually large for a pastel painting, making the figures approximately life-size and enabling the artist to include a vast range of detail, especially in the faces and clothing.

▼ **BARRY ATHERTON**
PORTRAIT OF A PAINTER
The informal pose and studio background give the figure both character and context. The dark clothing creates a solid shape, bringing the subject out clearly from the background, but even the darkest tones are alive with touches of vivid colour, every mark playing an active role in modelling the forms and creating texture.

▼ **TOM COATES**
WOMAN IN PINK
Although the technique used in this study is free and sketchy, using a range of linear marks, hatching and shading to structure and round out the forms, it creates a precise and powerful description of its subject. The limited colour range provides tonal contrast and local colour.

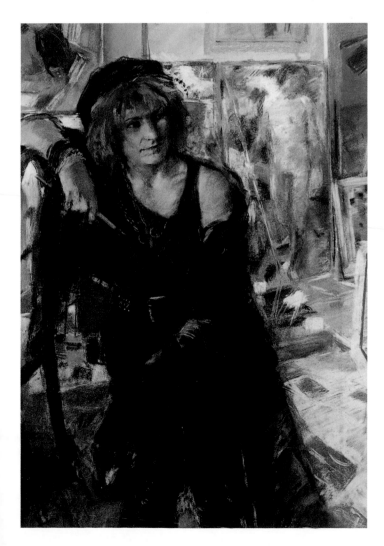

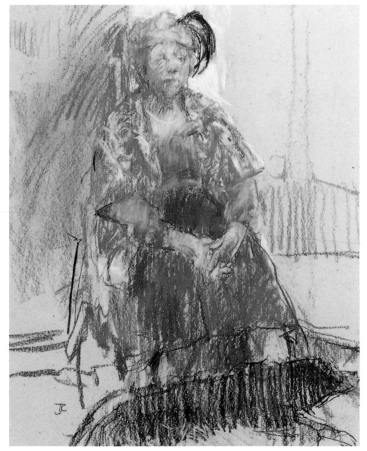

Lighting

Pastel is an excellent medium for rendering dramatic qualities of light in a portrait. The bright colours and scintillating pale tones lend themselves to intense highlights and splashes of strong illumination. For a heavy chiaroscuro effect, the pastel technique of working on a coloured ground (see page 12) is extremely effective. If you use a mid-toned base, you can work up the extremes of tonal values using your darkest and brightest pastel colours, while maintaining a coherent overall scheme.

An almost monochrome approach creates a strong sense of mood, with any small touches of pure colour serving to emphasize the tonal interpretation. However, while you do need some contrast of tonal values to convey dramatic lighting, you can also make use of strong colour interactions to model the illuminated form – for instance, complementary contrasts such as red/green or yellow/mauve, and variations between warm and cool colours or gentle and acid hues.

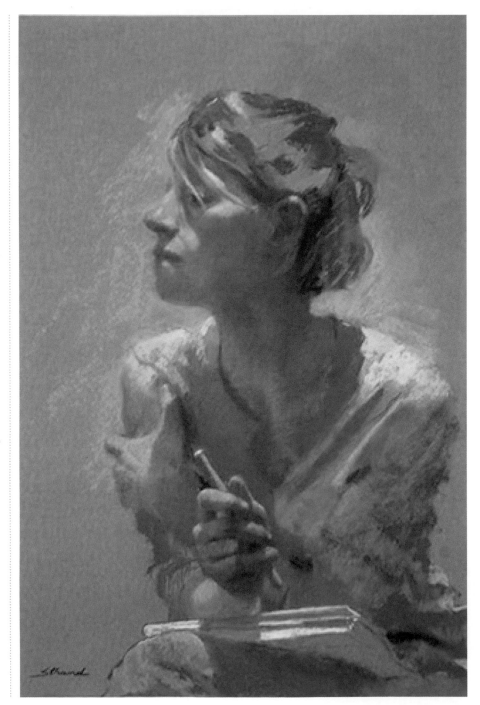

◄ **SALLY STRAND**
KARI
This is a contemplative portrait in which soft sidelighting creates subtle shadows on the face and hands. Despite the quiet mood, the use of complementary colours – the turquoise top and the touches of orange in the hair – gives the portrait great vibrancy.

► **LUVERNE LIGHTFOOT**
STRAW HAT
The open weave of the straw hat in this portrait creates lovely dappled shadows on the face. The artist began by making a watercolour underpainting to establish the areas of light and shade; soft pastel strokes were then applied on top while still allowing some of the underlying paint to show through, creating exciting colour vibrations.

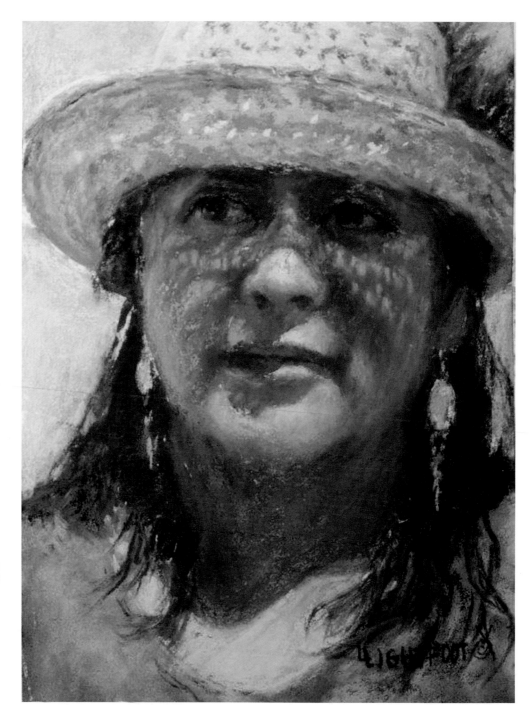

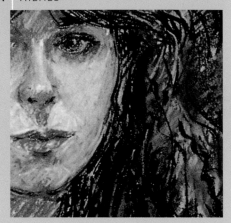

Demonstration

....

Kay Gallwey

This portrait has an expressive gestural quality that records the artist's confident approach to the medium. While enjoying the freedom of a bold, calligraphic technique, she has achieved a remarkably true likeness of the subject.

Arranging the pose

The artist has chosen to create colour interest by swathing the sitter in a patterned shawl and posing her against the backdrop of a decorative curtain. This gives a very rich surround that enhances the dramatic contrast of the pale skin tones and dark hair. The artist's easel is set up at an angle that enables her to see both the sitter and the drawing at the same time, so that her observations are quickly and directly transferred to the paper.

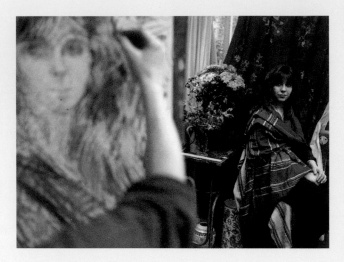

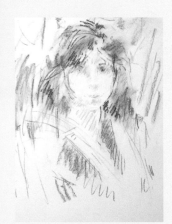

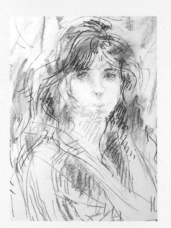

2 The artist relies on the calligraphic quality of the pastel marks to develop the detail of the portrait. From the increasingly dense network of coloured lines the modelling of face and hair emerges more clearly. The eyes are already quite sharply defined, as these are always a focal point in a portrait.

3 The range of tones and colours is extended overall, in some places boldly stated and in others subtly blended by finger rubbing.

1 The general shapes of head, hair, face and upper body are loosely blocked in with bold linear marks and hatching In places, the pastel is spread by the movement of the artist's hand and by deliberate rubbing with the fingers. This initial, sketchy stage creates a general impression of the local colours in each element of the portrait. The darker pastel colours are used to define the basic structure of the head.

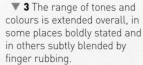

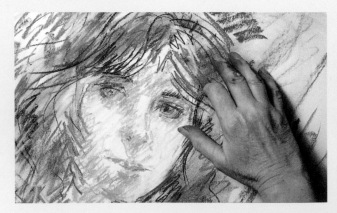

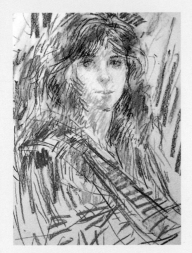

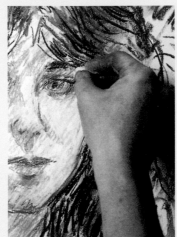

▲ **4** The whole surface is kept active at every stage. Although the use of colour is now more elaborate, the rendering remains open and workable due to the loose weaving of strokes.

▲ **5** The modelling of the face and variation of the flesh tints is developed more intensely. Luminous highlighting is applied to the eyes and the projecting curves of the face.

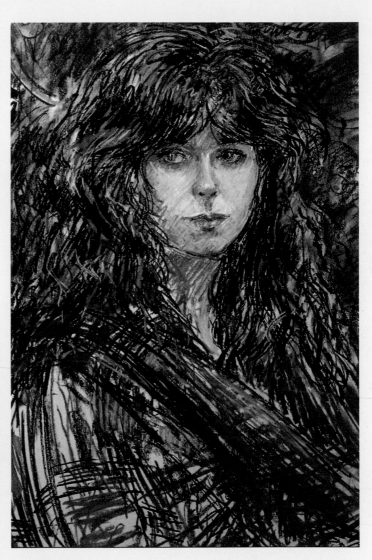

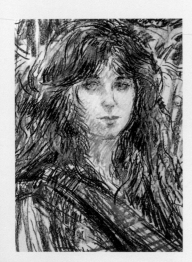

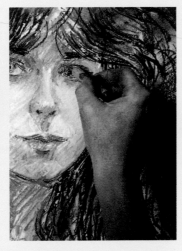

▲ **6** Strong directional lines describe the flowing hair, the colours providing greater contrast of tone. A similar treatment is applied to the folds of the patterned shawl.

▲ **7** Having added mid-toned greys and mauves to the shadowing around the eye sockets and nose, the artist adds crisp finishing touches that bring back the focus and clarity of the eyes.

▲ KAY GALLWEY
PORTRAIT OF STEFANIE

Animals

The range of pastel techniques – linear strokes, broken colour, feathering, hatching and stippling – makes the medium ideal for representing animal textures. It is suited not only to the highly tactile qualities of fur and feathers, but also to the baggy, rough skins of animals such as the elephant and rhinoceros, and the smooth-haired hides of horses and cattle. As a dynamic colour medium, pastel readily accommodates bold markings such as spots and stripes, the vivid colour schemes of tropical birds and the jewelled patterning of fish scales or snake skin.

Ways and means

Because animals rarely pose, most artists find it difficult, at least at first, to draw from the living model. The obvious solution seems to be using photographs, and this certainly widens the choice of creatures you can study at close quarters and avoids the problem of the animal walking away before you can put pastel to paper. However, a static photographic image can be lifeless and lacking in detail. Where it is essential to work from photographs, be sure to allow your technique plenty of life of its own to convey your interest in the subject.

Study and practice

Pets are the easiest live models to start with, or farm or zoo animals, depending on accessibility. When studying the real thing, you may find it helpful at first to spend at least as much time watching the animal as you do drawing it. Give yourself time to get used to the continual movement so that you can start to identify the animal's characteristic details of form and texture.

If you want to put in some practice on describing detail, you can work from stuffed museum exhibits; some artists even use dead animals and birds found in good condition. This enables you to study pattern and texture closely and unhurriedly, and to observe the ways a creature's markings relate to its physical structure. Anatomical studies are not essential to animal drawing, unless you want to take a scientific interest.

Bear in mind that the most detailed drawing of an animal is not necessarily the most realistic. When you look at a cat, a giraffe, or a bullfinch, you do not take in every hair, every colour patch, every barb on a feather. A drawing or painting is always as much about your own perception as it is about the sum total of your subject.

▶ JUDE TOLAR
PASTURE PALS
In this charming scene, our eye follows the direction of the horse's gaze down to the tiny bird in the grass – so small that it is easy to miss at first glance. Scumbled and broken colour are used to great effect to convey the scrubby texture of the ground; bold strokes pick out the colours and add texture to the horse's mane and tail.

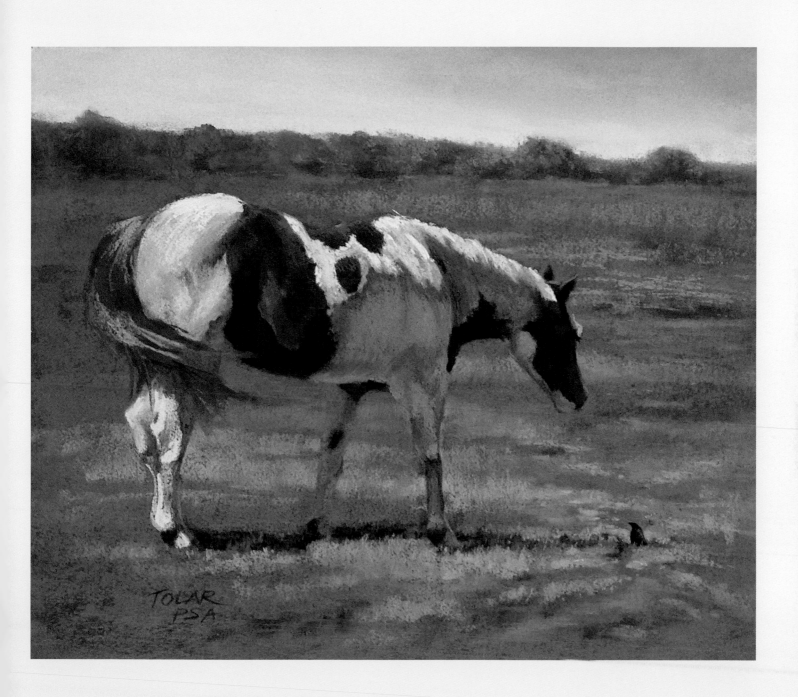

Sketches

When you are working from live models, quick sketches are an invaluable method of getting to know animal forms. The free motion of a pastel stick enables you to respond very quickly to the movements of the subject, and you do not have the pressure to produce a highly finished image – a single continuous line sometimes catches the perfect impression of a graceful animal contour. Many sketches are just as satisfying in their own terms as are more lengthy and considered works.

Sketching sidesteps the problem of getting enough time to study the animal effectively, because your representations can be a series of rapid drawings, or you can have several sketches on the go and return to the appropriate one according to what the animal is doing at any given time. Domestic and zoo animals develop routine movements and cycles of behaviour, so that you can count on an individual pose or movement recurring. With patience you will begin to recognize the elements that are essential to your representation, and develop effective ways of interpreting them in pastel.

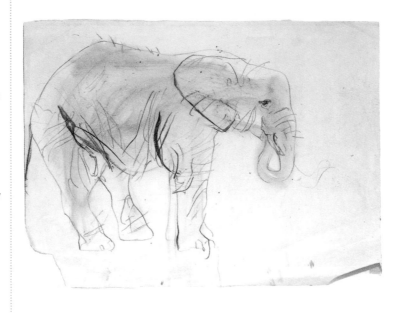

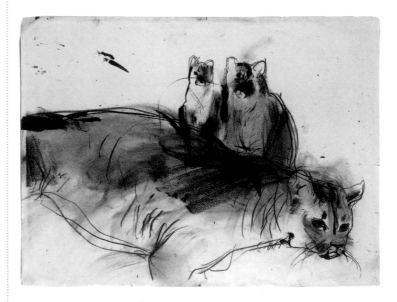

◀ STAN SMITH
"ELEPHANT" AND "COUGARS"
In these two sketches, the lines are loosely worked in oil pastel (part of the elephant's outline is in pencil), and the washed colour is laid in with oil paint thinned with turpentine. The rapid movements of the pastel strokes show how quickly the sketches were drawn, focusing on the contours and skin texture of the animals' bodies, and including only the most essential features.

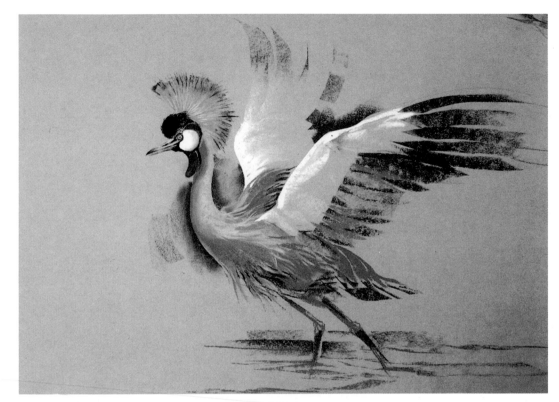

▶ JOHN BARBER
CRANE
Different types of pastel marks
can be matched to the range of
textures in an animal or bird. In
this soft pastel sketch, the artist
has used broad side strokes to
define the sweeping shapes of
body and wings (see detail below),
fine linear marks for the crest and
smaller body feathers, and gentle
blending to recreate the soft sheen
of the downy plumage on the bird's
neck and breast.

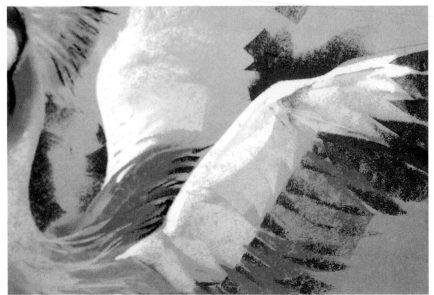

Studies

A study is a much more detailed rendering than a sketch, typically requiring plenty of time for a rigorous visual analysis focusing on the exact form and texture of the animal. It is, in effect, a portrait, or likeness of the particular animal, whereas a sketch may be more freely concerned with the essential characteristics of the species and how these are displayed in typical poses and movements.

Working with pastel, you need to build the image patiently with gradual layering of many individual marks. You need time to do this, which almost certainly means that you will have to refer to photographs, as the animal will not maintain one pose for long. Ideally, you should combine live observation with photographic reference, so that your memory supplements the pictorial record. It is far preferable to take your own photos of a living creature than to work from pictures in books or magazines, and you can also use sketches as reference, taken from the model, a practice that enables you to relate your observations to the technical solutions that your medium can provide.

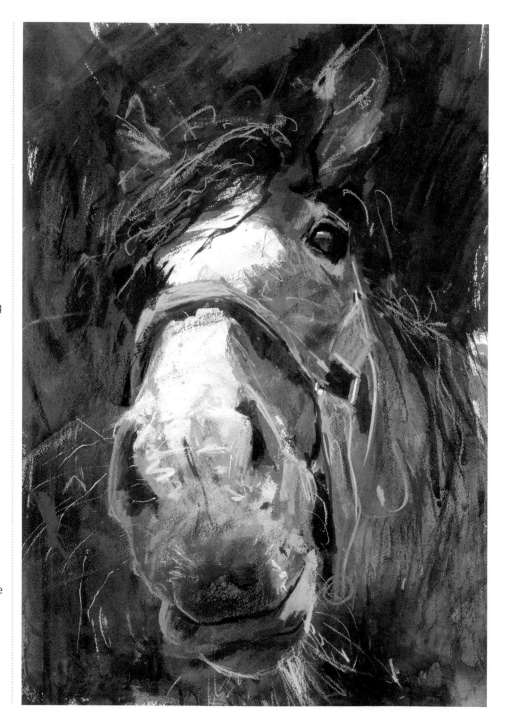

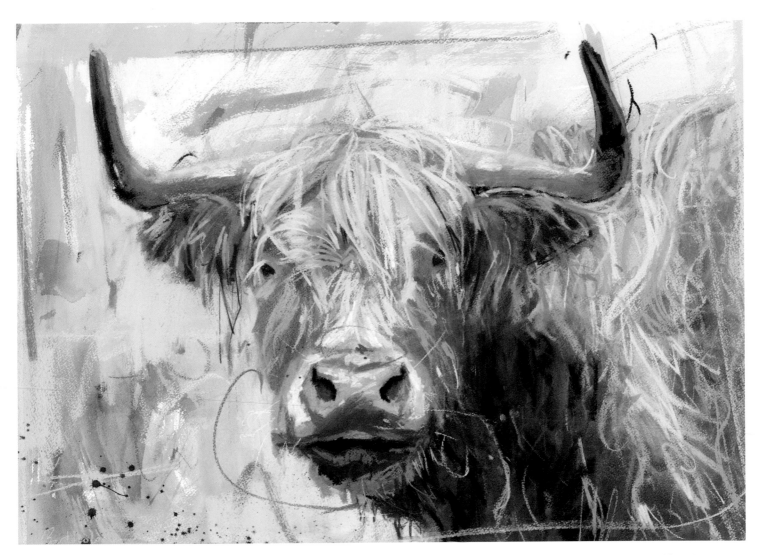

◀ JAMES BARTHOLOMEW
HORSE IN THE BLUE HALTER
Pastel is a wonderful medium for capturing the soft texture of a horse's hide. Here, the artist has taken care not to overblend the colours: underlying colours and the tooth of the paper show through in places, contributing to the texture. The viewpoint, looking up at the horse, emphasizes its size.

▲ JAMES BARTHOLOMEW
MORAG
Spontaneous gestural marks and sweeping strokes of pastel over a watercolour underpainting give this work tremendous life and vibrancy. The pale blue background complements the pink and orange colours of the cow's flowing strands of hair.

Birds

Birds are a wonderful subject for drawing and painting. They present a huge variety of form, size, texture and colour, from the compact bodies and discreet earthy colouring of ordinary garden species to the exuberant wings and crests and brilliant colours of tropical birds. There is also a stunning visual difference between a bird on the ground or perched on a branch and the same bird in flight with its wings fully extended.

Some artists specialize in bird studies and can spend all their working lives discovering the many variations on the theme. If you want to make this an area of special interest, you can gather reference from a range of sources. First, and most importantly, you can observe and sketch birds in the wild. Details of form, colour and texture can be gleaned from photographs, and also through museum studies of stuffed specimens. Exotic species can be seen live in enclosed aviaries, and you can again supplement your knowledge of them with photographic reference. There are many books describing the anatomical detail and flight mechanisms of birds, which can all add to your understanding of the subject.

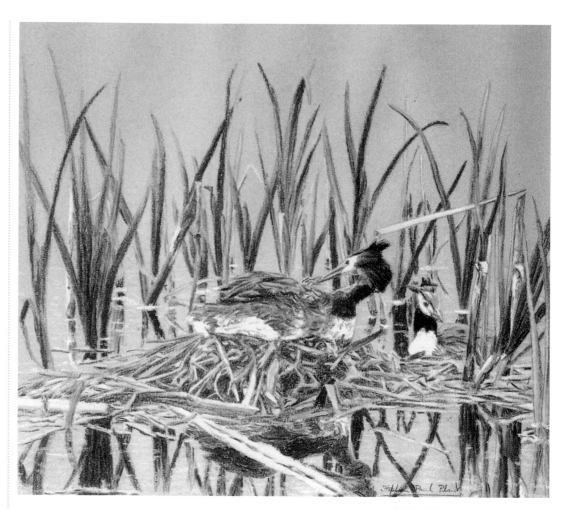

▲ STEPHEN PAUL PLANT
GREAT CRESTED GREBES
There is an interesting contrast in the rounded shapes of the birds' bodies and the elongated forms of the crested heads with their long, pointed bills. The paper colour creates a unified tone that assists in the impression of the birds being partially camouflaged in their habitat.

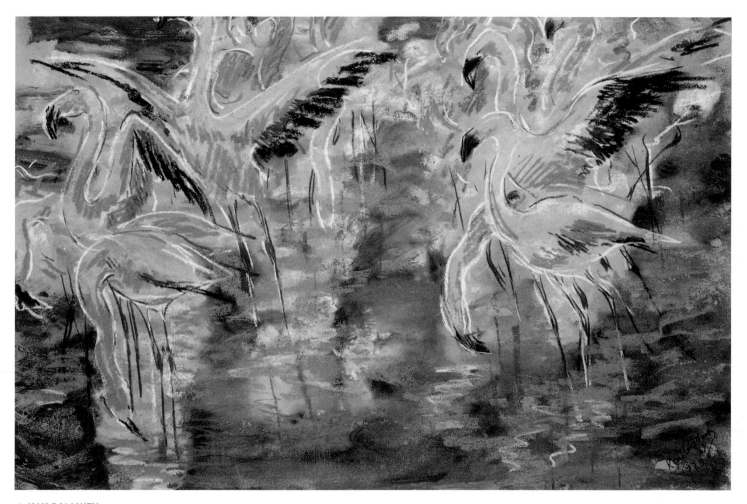

▲ KAY GALLWEY
FLAMINGOES
The fluid areas of colour that
establish the general shapes of the
birds and the dark ground of the
water surface were created by
"printing off" a loosely worked oil
painting onto paper. The oil colour
was allowed to dry before the
linear detail of the birds was freely
drawn with bold pastel colours.
Pastel strokes also describe the
shimmering reflections of the
flamingoes' colours on the water.

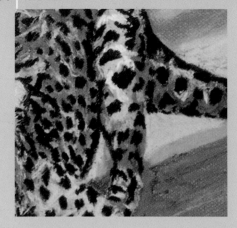

Demonstration

Judy Martin

To draw an image of this kind from life is obviously impossible. The photograph used as reference was a very dynamic shot, and the incomplete pose, with tail and foreleg cropped, was retained as appropriate to the sense of movement conveyed by the image. The artist had previously studied cheetahs in sketches made at the zoo.

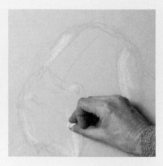

▲ **1** The artist is particularly interested in the camouflage patterns of animals. The sandy colour of the paper forms the base colour both of the cheetah's fur and the dry, earthy background. The contours are freely sketched in yellow ochre and the highlight areas blocked in with a paler yellow tint.

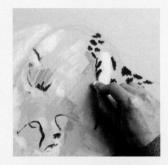

▲ **2** Some of the cheetah's markings are drawn in black pastel to key in the darkest tones. Yellow, orange and brown tints in the fur are loosely indicated with rapid shading and broad, short side strokes.

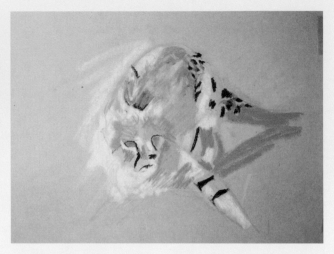

▲ **3** The patches of light and shade surrounding the animal are blocked in, and further tones and colours added to the fur, using gestural marks made with the pastel tip. The hints of colour are overstated at this stage, but will become more integrated with gradual overworking.

▼ **4** The artist begins to define the head, using the natural pattern of black lines around the eyes and nose, and the dark tufts behind the ears. With the stronger blacks in place, the colour detail is reworked more heavily, including the orange and gold eyes.

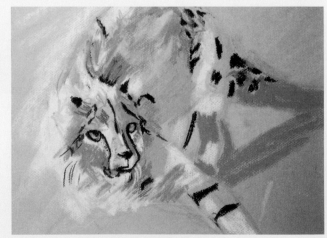

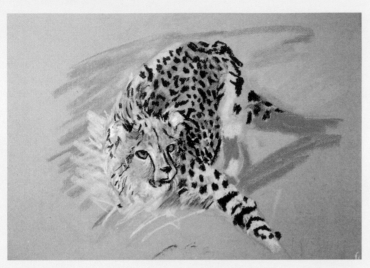

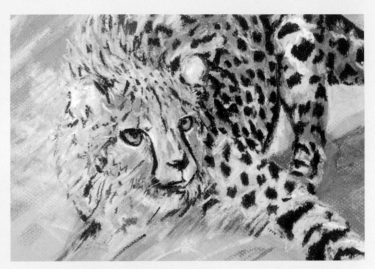

▲ **5** The pattern of spots on the cheetah's body and ringed markings on the foreleg are thickly worked with the pastel tip. Around the black spots, the colour detail is developed with shading the linear marks, including the white fur highlighting the head and face.

▼ **6** The cast shadow under the body and tail is emphasized with a cold grey that contrasts with the warm yellows. The sunlight reflecting on the ground plane is similarly strengthened with the same pale yellow tint previously applied to the fur.

▲ **7** The final steps are to put finishing touches to the colour detail. Because the yellows now appear a little flat, stronger orange and red ochre patches are laid into the body and tail, and the spot pattern is reworked in black and sepia. The ruff of fur around the head is more heavily textured.

▼ **JUDY MARTIN**
CHEETAH

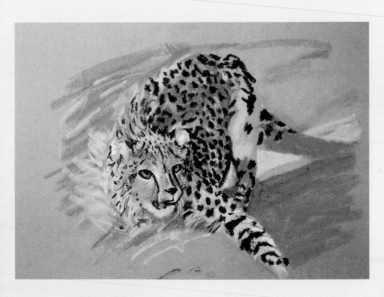

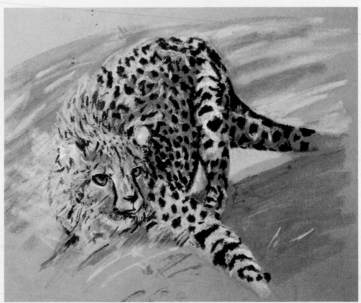

Still Life

The great advantage of still life is that you can choose a subject entirely within your control — unlike a person or animal, it doesn't walk away; unlike landscape subjects, it does not bend with the breeze or change character when the sun goes in. You can use a still life for a period of extended study, resulting in just one pastel rendering or many, so it is an excellent vehicle for learning your craft and sharpening your powers of observation.

Subjects

Natural objects readily present themselves as elements of still life because they have distinctive forms and varied colours and textures that give you plenty to work on at a relatively small scale — flowers, fruit and vegetables are the most obvious and perhaps most commonly chosen candidates. For the same reasons, domestic objects with reflective or patterned surfaces, such as bowls, jugs, pans and bottles made of metal, ceramic or glass are favourite components of still life. Often fabric is introduced, such as a tablecloth or curtain, to give a soft contrast to solid forms.

Less obvious, but equally promising subjects can be found randomly anywhere around the home — clothes and shoes, furniture, cushions and rugs, books and ornaments, garden tools, or brushes and pencils stored in jars in your studio. Any of these objects can be deliberately arranged, or you can treat them as "found groupings" and just study them as they are.

Variations

The scale of such still lifes is sympathetic for pastel work, but you need not be restricted to the domestic context. Different but equally "still" subjects come from the absence of human activity in normally busy scenes — empty deck chairs by the riverside or sea front, small boats tied to a dock, machinery on a building site standing idle outside working hours. There are also natural and man-made features in the landscape that provide outdoor still-life constructions — rocks and stones, for instance, or fences, walls and gateways. Such subjects incorporate many interesting elements of shape, form, colour and texture.

Whether you are drawing one object or many, and whatever scale you are working to, the active qualities of the marks you make with pastel can contribute a special character to the rendering. Be prepared to experiment with technique and try out alternative solutions — even a simple arrangement of two or three fruits can be interpreted in a variety of ways.

▶ LUVERNE LIGHTFOOT
TEAL VASE
This simple-looking still life is a lovely study in texture. The subject is lightly sketched with pastel pencil and then randomly sprayed using a water-filled spray bottle, creating random water patterns. Pastels are applied quickly to the wet and dry areas. This produces interesting colour mixes, variations and exciting textures.

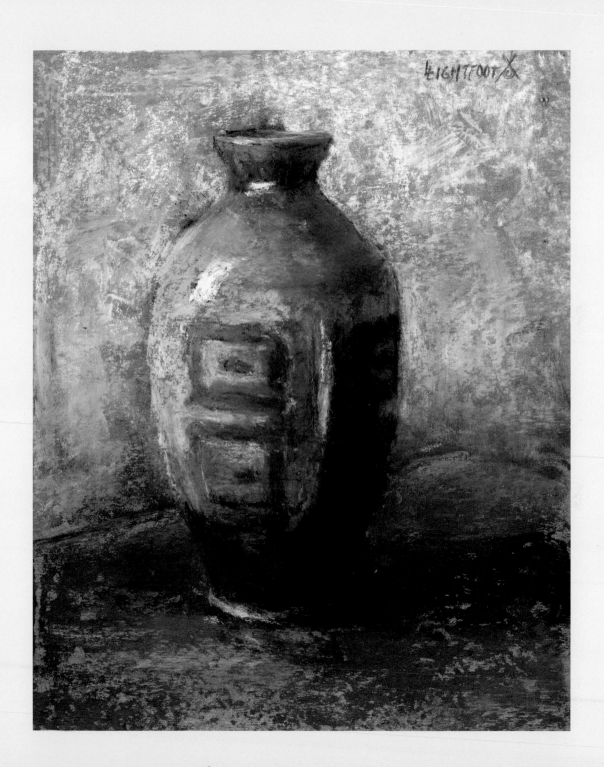

Fruit and Vegetables

The great variety of fruit and vegetables gives you a choice of many different qualities of form, colour and texture. You can focus on the sculptural elements of volume and contour, modelling the forms with subtle gradations of light and shade, or you can emphasize the colours and textures, working the pastel marks into an almost abstract pattern that incorporates all the variations of surface detail.

Depending on your approach, you may want to isolate the subject and treat it as a self-contained form, or you may prefer to give it a context that includes other objects and a recognizable background. When you are working with simple forms, the quality of light is important – angled light will emphasize the structure of the object, whereas an even spread of light may flatten the forms and reduce the range of visual interest.

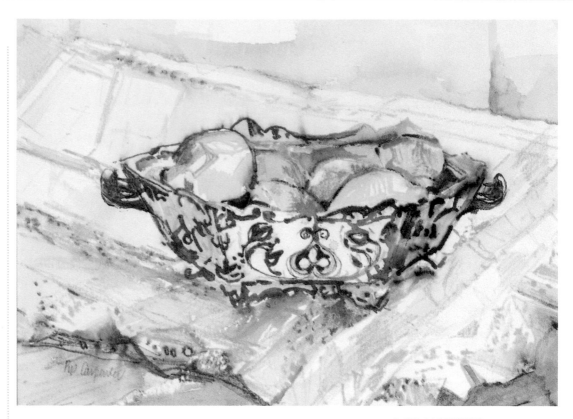

▲ PIP CARPENTER
BOWL OF LEMONS
This is an interesting use of water-soluble pastel, some parts of the image being drawn with the dry sticks, others by dipping the pastel into water and drawing with the wet tip. This is combined with loose washes of watercolour that define shadow areas and local colour.

◄ SALLY STRAND
LEMONS
The simple shapes in this composition are a strong vehicle for the artist's exceptional skill as a colourist. Each of the lemons is modelled with a range of subtle hues, from warm yellow and pink to cold blue, green and lilac. The effect of brilliant sunlight derives from bold definition of the highlight areas.

▼ LISA OBER
TWO BEETS OR NOT TWO BEETS
Every tiny detail in this photorealistic drawing has been painstakingly observed, from the delicate veining on the leaves to the tiny highlights on the beets, and the image built up from layer upon layer of overlaid colour. Although the arrangement looks artless, it takes time to get something like this just right – the negative spaces are just as important as the objects themselves.

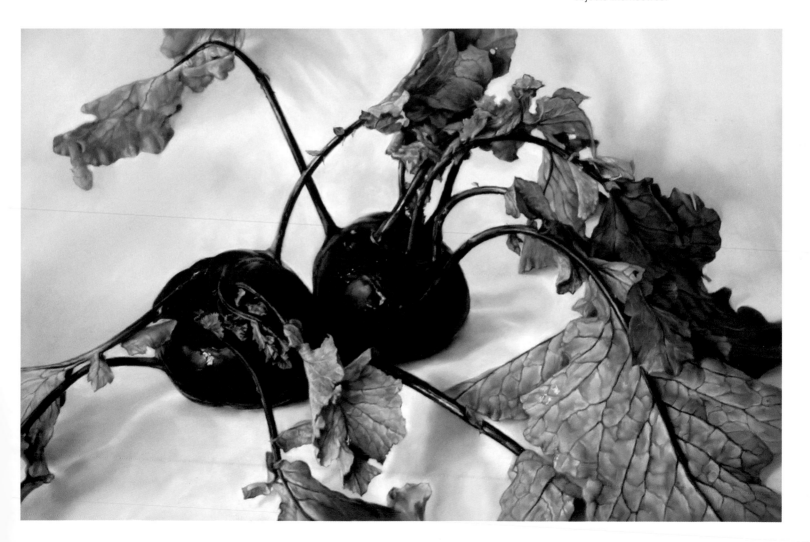

Pattern

Many still life groupings provide a wealth of pattern elements, both in the juxtaposition of varied shapes and forms and in the flat patterns often used to decorate domestic items such as containers, ornaments and furnishing fabrics.

Because you can treat pastel as a medium of line or of mass, it is particularly well suited to pattern-making. Distinct pattern elements can be drawn with the pastel stick, using outlines and linear marks to describe individual shapes and surface details. Colour areas can be laid in as solidly shaded, blended or broken colour. Use the mark-making capabilities of the pastel to match specific elements of your subject.

Imposed patterns, such as glazed decoration on ceramic ware or printed fabric patterns, are designed to create a colourful surface effect, an element that adds liveliness to your rendering. In a still life, however, they are not seen plainly as flat patterns but as an additional element of form. You may notice how the imposed pattern can describe something about the underlying structure of the patterned object or material – distortion of the pattern as it wraps around a bowl or jug, for instance, or breaks in continuity that signify fabric folds.

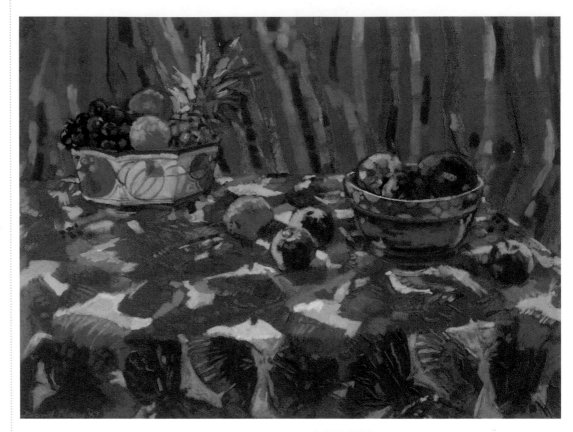

▲ DAVID NAPP
FABRICS AND FRUIT
Working with a palette like this, in which dense, highly saturated hues predominate, it would be easy to lose control of form and structure in the composition. Here the artist moves confidently between flat surface patterns and colour characteristics that describe three-dimensional volumes. By accurately identifying specific shapes and the colour values they contain, he is able to organize the image effectively without dimming the dramatic impact of its glorious hues.

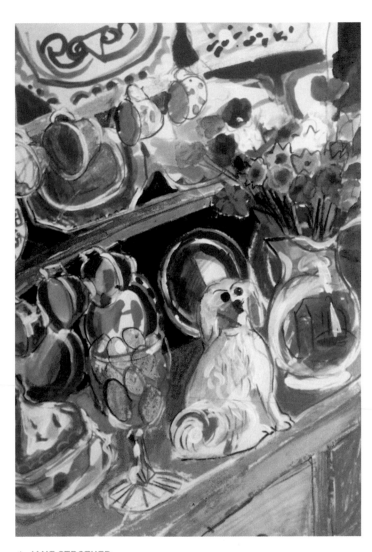

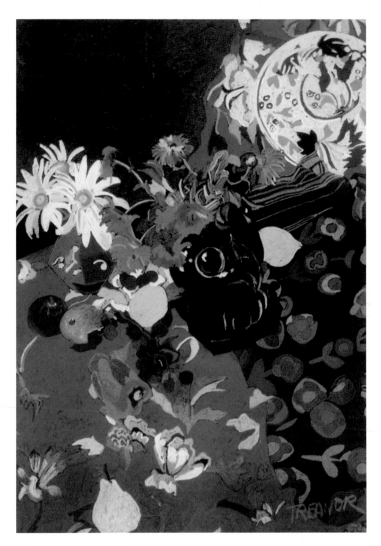

▲ JANE STROTHER
WELSH DRESSER
Oil pastel is used freely to draw
the framework of the image, with
watercolour to fill in colour detail.
The pastel acts as a resist (see
Resist Techniques, page 44)
breaking through the fluid paint.
The varied objects and their
pattern elements are unified by
the strong colour theme.

▲ FRANCES TREANOR
PANDORA DREAMING
The patterns are deliberately
varied to create strong oppositions
of colour and shape, but the
intensity of the pastel colour is a
cohesive factor in the composition.
An interesting device is the
contrast of natural with stylized
flower forms.

Groups

A grouping of objects can either be a deliberate arrangement or a "found" group that needs little or no alteration. Once you start to look around for a subject to draw, you will find many accidental arrangements around your home that provide pleasing material for a pastel rendering, such as plants on a windowsill, plates and glasses on a table, books and ornaments on the shelves. Sometimes you may need to adjust a found subject slightly, to get a better profile on an interesting shape, for instance, or to make sure the light strikes the subject at an illuminating angle.

A basic element of any still life group is the relationships of form and space. Whether the objects you select are similar or different in individual character, their shapes and forms interact, and occupy an area within their surroundings. You may choose to indicate the location of the still life simply – just a couple of lines can suggest the area of space created by a vertical and a horizontal plane, such as a tabletop and background wall. If you give it a more detailed context – seen against the furnishings of a room, for instance, or a view through the window – you have many more visual elements to play with.

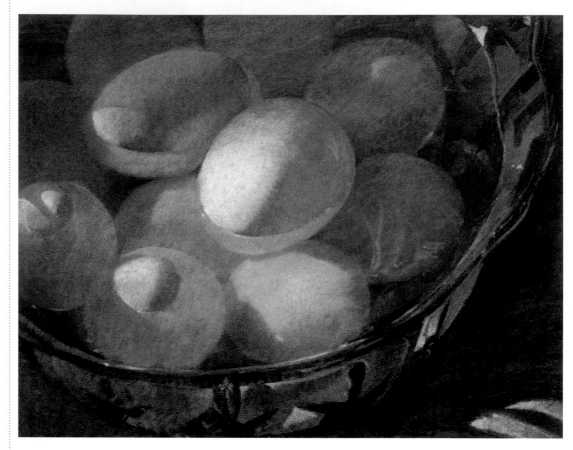

▲ **SALLY STRAND**
BOWL OF EGGS
By putting together ordinary domestic objects in an inventive way, the artist finds an unusual and beautiful image. The repetitive, simple volumes of the eggs are subtly disrupted by the water level in the bowl. There is a fascinating contrast between the opaque, smooth eggshells and the reflective transparency of water and cut glass, fully brought out by the handling of the pastel marks to indicate different qualities of surface texture and colour. But the success of the image is dependent as much on highly developed skills of observation as on expert handling of the medium.

▶ LISA OBER
STANDING ROOM ONLY
These glass bottles are a
challenging subject, with myriad
nuanced reflections, highlights
and subtle colour transitions. The
composition has been carefully
arranged to exploit the interlocking
and overlapping shapes.

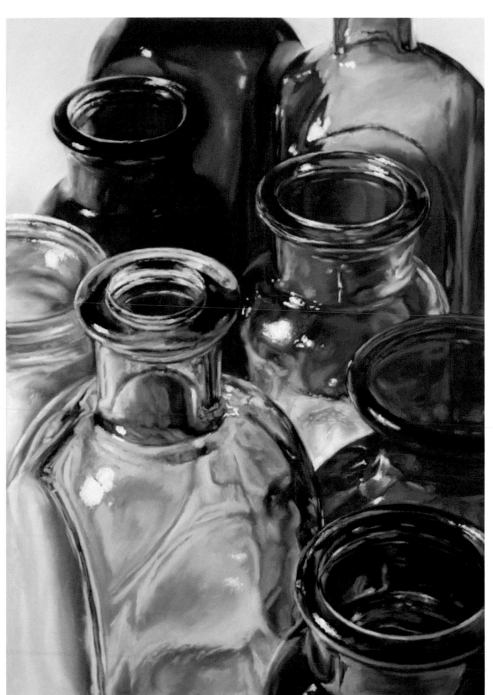

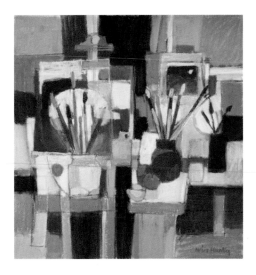

▲ MOIRA HUNTLY
STUDIO II
The easels and jars of brushes are
treated as simple geometric shapes
and blocks of colour, and the
interest is as much in the way these
shapes overlap and complement
each other as it is in the objects
themselves.

Interior Still Life

A furnished room is in itself a still life, and any aspect of it may provide your subject. A partial view of a room will include interesting groupings of objects seen in diminishing scale, both in their actual sizes and in the spatial relationships arising from the perspective of the room.

The focal point of the arrangement could be a vase of flowers on a table, but this will be seen as a relatively small element in comparison with, say, the table on which it stands. You need to consider how the marks you make on paper can represent the varying degrees of detail that you can identify from your chosen viewpoint.

An important aspect of interior still life is the quality of light. You can work by artificial light, but there are practical drawbacks. A central or overhead light is designed to illuminate the whole room, so it may give a too-even, flat quality that deadens the subject. A lamp focused on the still life can provide a dramatic quality, but leaves you little light to work by. Some compromise between the two may be the answer to this problem.

Many artists prefer to work by natural light from a nearby window. Light directed from a single source helps to model form, and daylight entering a room also provides distinctive colour qualities – the gold light of a summer afternoon, for instance, or the cold grey light of a wintry day. When you are viewing a still life in context, these external factors contribute to the range of your interpretation.

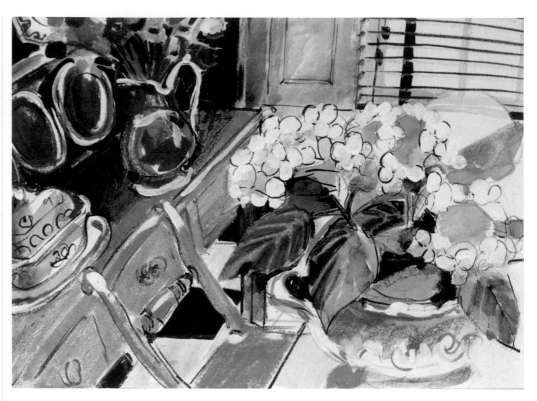

▲ JANE STROTHER
**WELSH DRESSER
AND HYDRANGEA**
An unusual perspective pulls the viewer right into the domestic setting, creating strong rhythms that lead the eye all around the image. The combination of watercolour paint and oil pastel is used even handedly, both media employed to develop linear structures and colour masses.

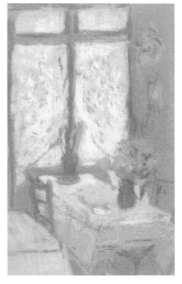

◀ CHARLOTTE ARDIZZONE
TABLE IN WINDOW
The simple planes of the composition focus interest in the quality of interior light. Each element is described as a colour mass, using harmonious hues punctuated with subtle complementary contrasts.

▼ MARGARET GLASS
MORNING LIGHT
In this detailed image, the artist has had to orchestrate various levels of information so that they become completely integrated. Accurate drawing was required to get the correct scale and perspective; there is a high degree of textural variety; and, as the title suggests, the relationships of colour and light are a central feature of the painting. These are developed by playing off warm and cool colours, to enhance the three-dimensional effect. The palette includes warm blues and greens and cold yellows, pinks and reds, reversing the colours' expected characteristics, and some of the shadow areas contain hues that are bright, but cool and recessive.

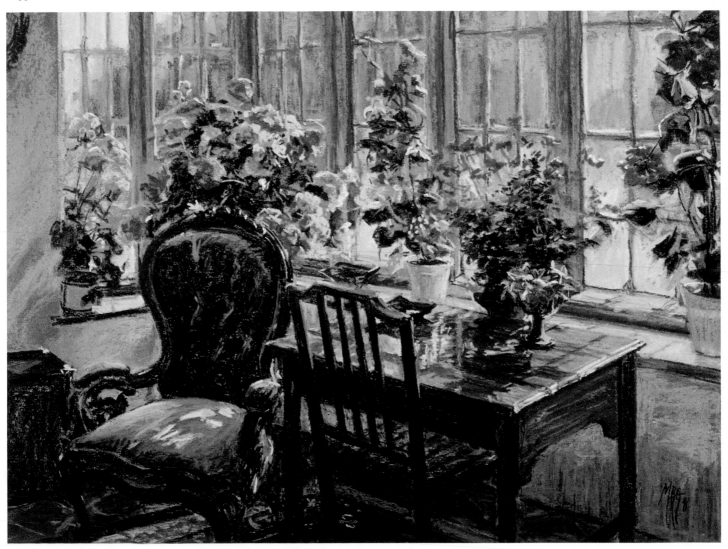

Exterior Still Life

The subjects included here stretch the traditional definition of still life groupings, but in the same way as the small-scale still life, they are a vehicle for investigating the formal and technical problems of pastel rendering and also a means of creating expressive images.

Outdoor subjects are most likely to fall into the category of "found" still life since your opportunity to rearrange the elements will be limited. This is useful discipline, as your subject may contain some aspect that you find difficult to tackle, giving you a problem of observation or interpretation that you might avoid if setting up a still life group yourself.

Be prepared to meet such challenges, and if it doesn't work out immediately, perhaps make some quick sketches that you can use as reference to try again on your return home.

There are practical drawbacks to working outdoors. If you haven't a camera with you, the time you can take to study the subject may be limited, so don't attempt an over-ambitious approach in terms of scale or technique. Also, of course, drawing in public does attract attention, which can be disconcerting even to experienced artists, but don't be put off by the idea that passers by may be critical of your work.

▶ JANE STROTHER
CONTAINER PLANTS
This attractive image is an illustration for reproduction in print. The more intricate line detail is worked in coloured pencil over oil pastel. The pastel is rubbed in places to create massed colour, with individual strokes used to delineate flower and leaf forms.

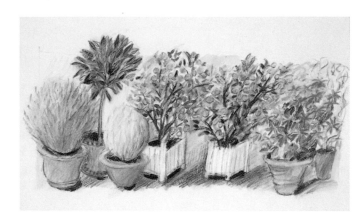

▼ KEITH BOWEN
STONE WALL
The close-up viewpoint features the abstract qualities of the wall, yet the degree of detail makes for a strong representational image, drawn in ink and soft pastel.

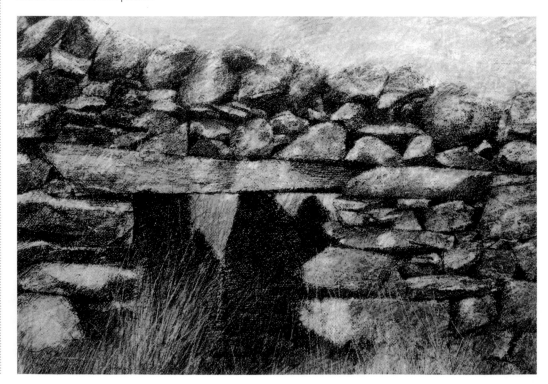

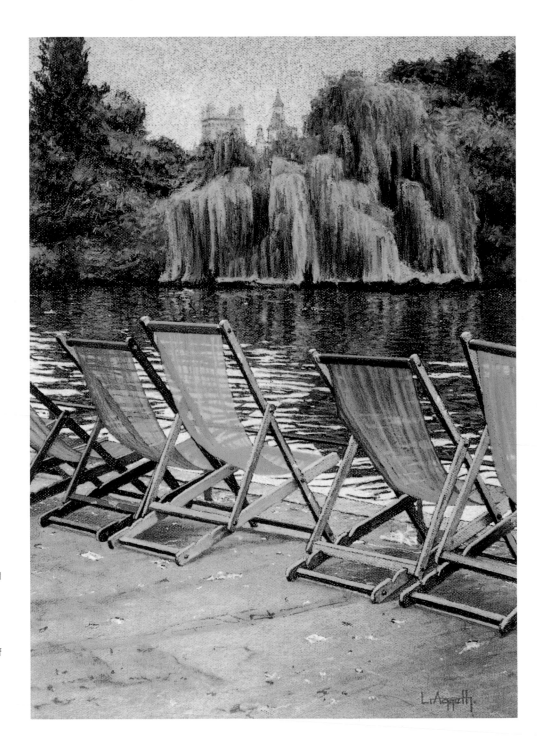

▶ **LIONEL AGGETT**
WEAR THE GREEN WILLOW
The repetitive shapes of the deckchairs form an interesting still-life group, sufficiently varied in their different heights and spacings to avoid a regimented effect. The colour values and directions of the pastel strokes have been expertly controlled to create the subtle translucence of the deckchair fabrics.

Flowers

Flowers are just about the perfect subject for pastel painting — there can be few pastellists who have not included flower subjects in their repertoire, and this is the ideal theme for the beginner. The brilliant colours of pastels match the richness of the natural flower colour range; the variations of texture that you can rapidly achieve with pastels correspond to the variety of flower forms — soft, smooth, folded, frilled, ragged, spiky.

Cut flowers arranged in a vase can be studied as individual forms or as a group. As in flower arranging, you can select the container to contribute a particular quality to the design — a decorative ceramic container gives a formal pattern quality that can be played off against the flower colours, while a glass vase both reflects the light and reveals the incidental detail of the massed flower stems. Outdoor subjects provide dense flower masses and changing nuances of colour, light and shade. An individual plant or a whole flower garden can be the inspiration for a free ßand enjoyable approach to pastel work.

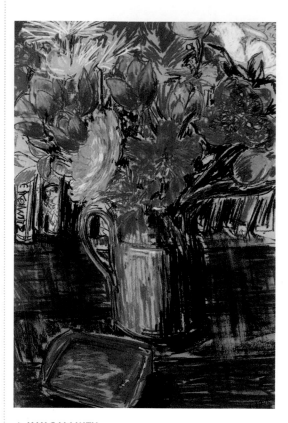

▲ KAY GALLWEY
SPRING FLOWERS IN BLUE JUG
Although the linear style of the pastel drawing allows for a very open, active surface, the individual shapes are boldly stated and modelled with strong colour and tone, conveying both the spatial arrangement of the group and the individual forms and textures.

▼ PIP CARPENTER
IRISES
Again in this image, the shapes and forms of the flowers are featured strongly, using an interesting technical sequence. The initial blocking in was done with a collage of coloured paper, washed over with watercolour to establish lights and shadows. Then water-soluble pastels were applied to intensify colours and create linear definition.

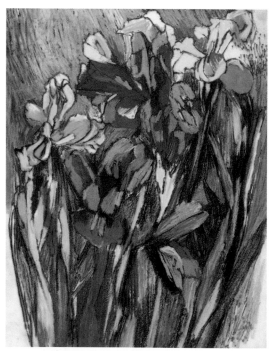

▶ CASEY KLAHN
FLUTED VASE, YELLOW
Oil bar, pastel and graphite are all used in this work. There is a lovely sense of life and movement in the drooping flower stems. The slightly reflective table top curves through the picture space and is balanced by the vertical lines in the background and in the fluted vase.

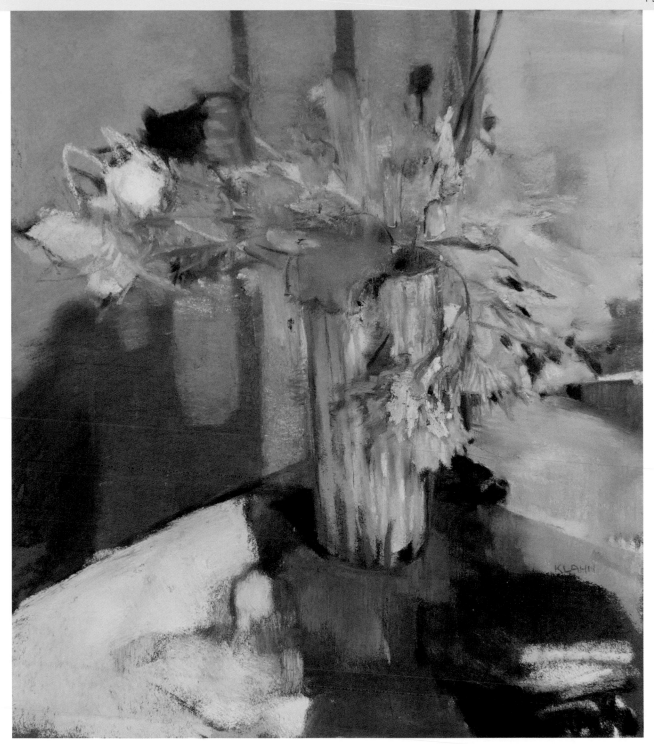

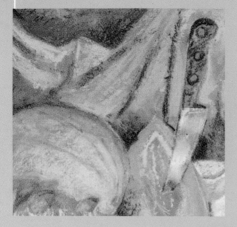

Demonstration

Rosalind Cuthbert

The luscious textures of cakes and fruits inspire a free, inventive way of working that combines a range of active techniques. The artist creates a vivid interplay of hues and tones within a strongly descriptive image.

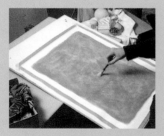

▲ **1** A textured ground is applied by brushing PVA (an adhesive acrylic medium) over stretched watercolour paper and rubbing in ground chalk (whiting) and raw umber pigment. The basic shapes of the still life are roughly sketched in white pastel, and the ground is reworked with a brush.

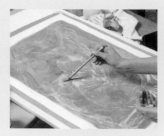

▲ **2** The outline sketch is developed in more detail, using sepia and light mauve to emphasize contours and suggest shadow tones, and pale tints to heighten individual shapes against the mid-toned background. By wet brushing over an application of yellow soft pastel the artist models the solid volumes of the fruits.

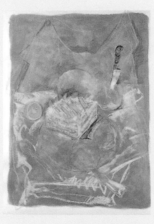

▲ **3** Working rapidly with a combination of linear marks and wet brushing, the artist blocks in several items of the still life more definitely. At this stage, the range of colours remains limited, and the drawing process is concentrated on developing form and texture.

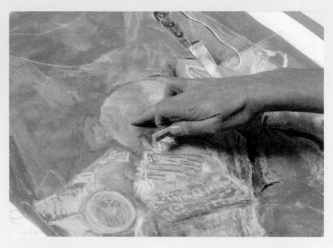

▲ **4** The palette is gradually extended by reference to local colours and the patterns of light and shade that model the forms. The colours are loosely blended by finger rubbing, maintaining an active surface effect.

▼ **5** Before continuing work on the central section of the image, the artist indicates the surrounding colours, laying in the strong white of the tablecloth more broadly, and indicating the warm red of the strawberry tart. She then returns to details of the fruits and cake.

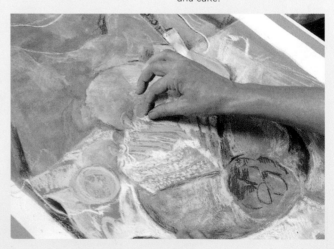

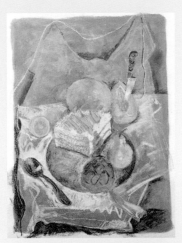

◀ **6** The image is now strongly established, but there is a lot of detail work to complete. The full range of tonal variations is in place but the forms and colours need to be built up with greater complexity.

▼ **7** As each component of the still life takes solid form, the artist works freely all over the image adding highlights and colour accents and strengthening the shadow areas. Dry pastel work is again combined with wet brushing to enhance the range of textures in the final image.

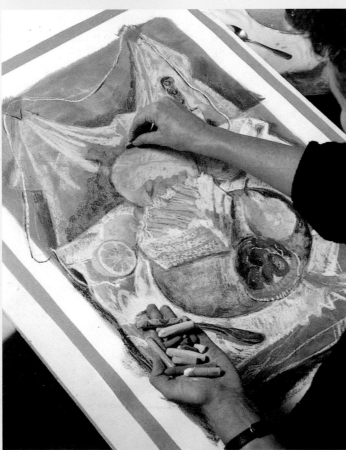

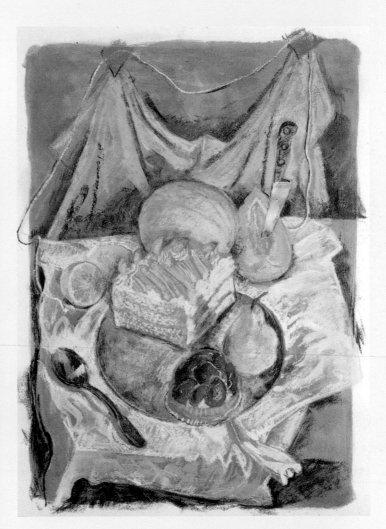

▲ ROSALIND CUTHBERT
THE FEAST

Index

Credits

Quarto would like to thank all the artists who kindly submitted work for this book, including the following who carried out demonstrations but are not credited in the captions:
David Carr, George Cayford, Patrick Cullen, Hazel Harrison, Ken Jackson, Judy Martin, Guy Roddon.

Aggett, Lionel.
Ardizzone, Charlotte.
Armfield, Diana.
Atherton, Barry. www.barryatherton.com
Baldwin, Janine. www.janinebaldwin.com
Barber, John. www.johnbarberartist.com
Bartholomew, James.
   www.jamesbartholomew.co.uk
Bowen, Keith. www.keithbowenartist.co.uk
Carpenter, Pip. www.pipcarpenter.co.uk
Cayford, George.
Coates, Tom.
Conley, Lynda. www.lyndaconley.com
Cullen, Patrick. www.patrickcullen.co.uk
Cuthbert, Rosalind.
Darlow, Les. www.lesdarlow.com
Demsteader, Mark.
   www.markdemsteader.com
Dulmes, Audrey. www.audreydulmesart.com
Elliot, John. www.johnelliot.com
Evans, Margaret. www.margaretevansart.com
Eyton, Anthony.
Ferry, David.
Forman, Zaria. www.zariaforman.com
Freeman, Barry.
Gallwey, Kay.
Glass, Margaret. www.margaretglass.com
Godsell, Brenda.

Hatts, Clifford.
Houser, John. www.jonhouser.co.uk
Huntlÿ, Moira. www.moirahuntly.com
Katchen, Carole. www.carolekatchen.com
Klahn, Casey. www.thecolorist.blogspot.com
Larlham, Margaret.
   www.margaretlarlham.com
Marsters, Geoff.
Martin, Judy.
   www.judymartinpainter.wordpress.com
Le Saint, Jean-François. www.lesaint.fr
Lightfoot, Luverne. www.luvernelightfoot.com
Manifold, Debra.
Mertz, Nancie King.
   www.nanciekingmertz.com
Michaels, Eric. www.ericmichaelsfineart.com
Napp, David. www.davidnappfineart.com
Neale, Chris. www.chrisneale.com
Ober, Lisa www.lisaober.com
Oliver, Alan. www.alan-oliver.co.uk
Ordman, Aline. www.alineordman.com
Parker, Vincent.
Plant, Stephen Paul.
Poucher, Nancy. www.nancypoucher.com
Prentice, David.
Smith, Stan.
Sparkes, Roy.
Spinale, Maureen. www.maureenspinale.com
Strand, Sally. www.sallystrand.com
Stride, Sally. www.sallyandjeffery.com
Strother, Jane. www.janestrother.co.uk
Tolar, Jude. www.judetolar.com
Treanor, Frances. www.francestreanor.com
Wagner, Jill. www.jillwagnerart.com
Wise, Irene.
Wood, Enid. www.enidwood.com

All step-by-step and still life photography are the copyright of Quarto Publishing plc. While every effort has been made to credit contributors, Quarto would like to apologize should there have been any omissions or errors – and would be pleased to make the appropriate correction for future editions of the book.

Photographers
All the photographs of the demonstrations were taken by Jon Wyand and Chas Wilder.

Cover credits
Bartholomew, James, front jacket tr (detail)
Le Saint, Jean-François, front jacket cl (detail)
Wagner, Jill, back jacket tr (detail)

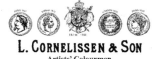

L. CORNELISSEN & SON
Artists' Colourmen
Suppliers of Materials for Painters, Gilders & Printmakers

With special thanks to L. Cornelissen & Son who supplied the featured tools and materials used in this book. Contact them at L. Cornelissen & Son, 105 Great Russell Street, London WC1B 3RY. For online enquiries, go to www.cornelissen.com.

Art Director: Caroline Guest
Designer: John Grain
Editorial Assistant: Danielle Watt
Picture Researcher: Nick Wheldon
Creative Director: Moira Clinch
Publisher: Samantha Warrington